Grades 4–8

AMERICAN HISTORY MATH

50 Problem-Solving Activities That Link Math to Key Events in U.S. History

Jacqueline B. Glasthal

We the Students

of Madison Middle School do heartily proclaim by signing and voting on this document that we agree with the right and responsibilities listed here. We will try as best we can to meet our responsibilities.

1. Putting all rulers and compasses ... after ... our.

ANN | CARLOS | KIM

SCHOLASTIC
PROFESSIONAL BOOKS

New York • Toronto • London • Auckland • Sydney

Dedication

*To my dad, who has shown me that, told correctly,
history is simply a story with some truth in it;
my brother, who has always known
that there is much more to mathematics than number-crunching;
my mom, from whom I've inherited patience—
at least for some things;
and Amy, who's got her entire future ahead of her
to make her mark on the world.*

Acknowledgments

*M*any people have supported and encouraged me during this effort, including many who couldn't imagine what types of links I might try to make between these two subjects, and others who couldn't figure out why in the world I would even want to try.

Special thanks to the "professional resources" that I relied upon, including Susan Drinan at the Atwater Kent Museum in Philadelphia, PA; George Deeming, curator of the Railroad Museum of Pennsylvania in Strasburg, PA; Adrienne L. Petrisko, assistant reference librarian at the Library Company of Philadelphia in Philadelphia, PA; and Tim Jones and Pam Sedowski at the Census Bureau. I would also like to extend a personal thanks to Sue Macy, who got me my day job; Barbara Nehmad, who actually sounded enthusiastic about helping me track down mileage facts about Christopher Columbus; Nick Flagg for making sure that my computer was always in good working order; Seán Crumley, for giving me Internet access; and my "big bro" for knowing enough about math to comment intelligently on my first draft.

I am also grateful to the staff of Scholastic *DynaMath*, from which I borrowed many resources—including the ideas for the money math and Harvey Girls activities—and to Terry Cooper, Virginia Dooley, and the rest of the Scholastic Professional Books staff for thinking of me and for giving me the opportunity to take a crack at this topic.

Cover design by Vincent Ceci and Jaime Lucero
Cover art by Tony DeLuna
Interior design by Kevin Callahan
Interior illustrations by Moffitt Cecil
Other art credits: Gale Research (38, 45 [Polk]); Library of Congress (6, 25, 45 [Jefferson]); Laurence Dunn (12)

ISBN 0-590-96568-9
Copyright © 1996 by Jacqueline B. Glasthal
All rights reserved.
Printed in the U.S.A.

12 11 10 9 8 7 6 5 4 3 2   7 8 9/9 0 1 2/0

Table of Contents

From the Author

Is it ***really true*** that history repeats itself? One aspect of history—the teaching of it—certainly does. Every year in classrooms throughout the country, students confront material that, just a year before, their teachers, or others like them, presented in a similar way to a different set of students. In American history, for example, a list of perennial topics would include the causes of the American Revolution, the meaning of the American flag and the Statue of Liberty, and the significance of famous Americans like George Washington and Benjamin Franklin. Some of the "basics" that are repeated annually in math classrooms appear in the form of explanations about how to add, subtract, multiply, divide, and use logic to solve problems.

In this book I attempt to combine these "givens" of mathematics and history and, by so doing, to propose new and creative ways to approach the two subjects. If you teach both math and history, the best ways to use this book will probably be quite obvious. When covering certain topics in American history with students, you could always refer to this book for possible math tie-ins. Or, if you're stuck for a novel way to teach symmetry, fraction addition, mental math, or how to round decimals, this book can also provide you with fresh ideas. If your emphasis is on only one of these subjects, the ideas can also be useful—although in some cases you may wish to alter them enough to keep the emphasis on your own area of specialization. Another option, of course, is to pair up with a history teacher if you teach math, or a math teacher if you teach history, and work together in both of your classrooms to present one or more of these project ideas.

I have organized the book chronologically by events in American history. To simplify use, each of the 11 chapters is structured around four recurring elements. "Historical Background" provides a short synopsis of the event. "So Where's the Math in That?" links the event with the math curriculum. "What to Do" suggests a set of steps to follow when presenting the main activity. Finally, "What Students Will Learn" describes the chapter's main learning objectives. Also provided within each section are related fun facts, ideas for extensions, and other resources that you may wish to use or share with your class.

As the teacher, of course, you should feel free to adapt, experiment with, or revise any or all of this material to best suit your own purposes. After trying an activity, you may wish to make notes to yourself about what worked, what didn't, and what you might do differently the next time you use it. As George Santayana, the Spanish-born American philosopher, once said, "Those who cannot remember the past are condemned to repeat it." My guess is that this statement applies as readily to education as it does to politics, government, and affairs of the heart.

—*J.G.*

1492
Columbus Sails West

Key Math Skills   Estimating rates of speed ☆ Whole number multiplication and division ☆ Graphing ☆ Averaging numbers

What You'll Need   Cardboard or posterboard ☆ Rulers ☆ Scissors
☆ A sink, tub, or large basin filled with an inch or two of water
☆ The leftover pieces from a few bars of soap ☆ Calculators

Historical Background

For many years, Christopher Columbus searched for a sponsor who would pay him to seek a westward water route to the Indies, the islands now known as Malaysia and Indonesia. Finally, in 1492, Queen Isabella and King Ferdinand of Spain agreed to finance the trip. What a weird feeling it must have been to sail west, not really knowing if he would ever spot land in the distance. When Columbus's crew of 90 men, in three ships, finally did reach land, after 33 days and nights on the water, they still had no idea where they were! Until his dying day, Columbus continued to believe that, since he had crossed the "Ocean Sea," he must have arrived somewhere in the Indies. He never dreamed that instead he had reached a different land mass, with some 11,000 sea miles (16,500 sea km) still separating him from his goal in the Far East.

So Where's the Math in That?

With only stars to guide them, how did Columbus and his crew know in which direction they were heading, or how many miles they had traveled? In large part they relied on a navigation technique known as dead reckoning. Every half hour a member of the crew would estimate each ship's speed, and then check the direction it was heading with a compass. This information was then noted on a small pegboard called a traverse. Later it was charted on a map.

The methods used to estimate speed were simple, but they were also crude. For example, one commonly used technique was to have a crew member drop a piece of wood into the ocean at the bow of the ship, and then time how long it took to reach the stern. In this activity, students will simulate this process. They will then compare the speed of their "toy boats" with that of the ships that Columbus sailed.

Christopher Columbus (1451–1506) made four voyages to the Caribbean.

AND DID YOU KNOW . . .

A nautical mile, equal to about 8,076 feet, is 1 percent longer than a land mile. No need to confuse your students, however. Let them calculate their distances in 5,280-foot land miles.

What to Do

1 Review with students what they already know about Columbus and his first voyage across the Atlantic. Fill in any gaps in their understanding with the information above. Then distribute a sheet of cardboard, a ruler, and a pair of scissors to each child. Direct each student to cut a 5-inch-long boat shape out of the cardboard, like the one shown below. In the back of their boats, be sure that each child has made a very thin cut. Explain that this is where the boat's "motor" (the piece of soap) will go.

Leave a thin notch for a sliver of soap (Step 1).

2 Fill a tub, basin, or the classroom sink with an inch or two of clean water. (To save time, break students into groups, and give each group its own tub.) Inform students that they will take turns testing their boats' speeds.

AND DID YOU KNOW . . .

Columbus believed that if he traveled 2,400 nautical miles due west from the Canary Islands he would reach Japan. That means he underestimated by about 8,200 nautical miles!

3 Explain that the soap propels the boats forward. (See "A Science Note to Teachers," on page 8.) To demonstrate, jam a small piece of soap into the cut made in the back of a sample boat, and set the boat in the water. At the same time, place one finger in the water, near the front of the boat.

4 Keeping your finger still, count the number of seconds it takes for the boat to float past your finger. (Use the "one one-hundred, two one-hundred, three one-hundred . . ." method of counting, or ask a student to watch the second hand on a clock for you instead.)

5 On the chalkboard, jot down the number of seconds it takes for the boat to move past your finger, as shown at right. (Remind students that the 5 inches refers to the length of the toy boat.)

> *My boat traveled 5 inches in 9 seconds.*

6 Once everyone in the class has had a chance to test his or her own boat's speed, take an informal survey to find out the range of the results. Then work as a class to average the times. If you'd like, have students graph these results.

7 Next, tell students that you are going to show them how to compare the speed of their own boats with the speed of the ships that Columbus sailed on. To do this, students will need to know these facts, which you should also write on the board:

> • *It took Columbus about 33 days—or 792 hours—to travel from Spain to the Bahamas. That's a distance of about 3,000 miles. (1 land mile = 5,280 feet)*
>
> • *Columbus's ships traveled an average speed of just under 4 miles (21,120 feet) per hour.*

8 Explain to students that, according to this last fact, Columbus's ships could travel about four miles in one hour. To compare this with the speed of their own boats, students will have to figure out about how far their own boats could travel in that time. The first step in doing this, you should explain, is to estimate about how far their own boats could travel in one minute—or 60 seconds. Ask for some suggestions about how they might figure this out. One way, for example, would be to keep multiplying the number of inches and seconds their boats traveled by the same number, as shown at the top of page 8.

AND DID YOU KNOW . . .
Columbus feared that his men would mutiny if they knew how far from Spain they had traveled. For this reason he kept a "false log," in which he recorded shorter distances than he truly believed they had gone. Ironically, the distances noted in this "false" log turned out to be more accurate than the distances that he believed to be true!

My boat can travel 5 inches in 9 seconds.

My boat can travel 10 inches in 18 seconds. (x 2)

My boat can travel 15 inches in 27 seconds. (x 3)

My boat can travel 20 inches in 36 seconds. (x 4)

My boat can travel 25 inches in 45 seconds. (x 5)

My boat can travel 30 inches in 54 seconds. (x 6)

My boat can travel 35 inches in 63 seconds. (x 7)

9 Since 63 seconds is close to 60 seconds, students can estimate that this sample boat could travel about 35 inches in that time.

10 Next ask students this: If their boat travels about 35 inches in one minute, about how far could it go in an hour? Bring students to the realization that, to answer this question, all they have to do is multiply the distance the boat could travel in a minute by 60, the number of minutes in an hour. This means that a toy boat that sails 5 inches in 9 seconds could go about 2,100 inches—or 175 feet—per hour.

11 Finally, using the facts about Columbus written on the chalkboard, challenge students to estimate about how long it would have taken their own boats to make the trip from Spain to North America.

What Students Will Learn

One way to solve the problem would be to figure out about how many hours it would take the toy boat to go the distance that Columbus's ships could travel in one hour. Students can then multiply that number by 792—the total number of hours that it took Columbus to cross the Atlantic Ocean.

Another method would be to divide the number of yards their toy boats traveled in one hour by 5,280,000—the number of yards in the one-way voyage from Spain to the Bahamas. (Hint: One yard is equal to three feet, or 36 inches.) Point out to students that in order to arrive at a reasonable estimate, it is crucial that they work with comparable units. A common error students might make would be to divide the number of *yards* their toy boats traveled by the number of *miles* that Columbus sailed.

To make their final answers more meaningful, encourage students to simplify their results by expressing them as days, months, and finally years. Then ask students to discuss how it would feel to travel on the open sea for that long.

A SCIENCE NOTE TO TEACHERS

Activities with "soap boats" are commonly used in science classes to demonstrate the concept of surface tension to students. The soap weakens the thin layer of "skin" on the top of the water, allowing students' boats to move fast. If you'd like, consult a science text for more information about surface tension. Then expand on this concept with your students. If they're interested, students can repeat this activity using cardboard boats of varying shapes and sizes to explore whether small boats or big boats tend to move faster. They can also try to determine if other variables, like the boat's shape, the material it's made from, or the size of the "soap motor," affect the speed.

Make Room for Columbus

No one knows for sure what the *Niña,* the *Pinta,* or the *Santa Maria* looked like. But experts do know that the *Santa Maria,* Columbus's flagship, was the largest of the three vessels. It was probably about 80 feet long and 23 feet wide, and it carried a crew of 40, including Columbus. (The *Niña,* Columbus's favorite of the three vessels, held 24 sailors, and the *Pinta* held the remaining 26 men.) To give kids a sense of the size of the *Santa Maria,* and of how crowded it would have been, work as a class to measure out a distance 80 feet long and 23 feet wide on your school playground. Mark the area with chalk, tape, or rope, and then ask 40 kids to stand in this space. Remind the class that the deck of the ship was also used to carry food, beverages, the crew's personal belongings, and other supplies. Since there was no room on board ship for beds, the men had to sleep anywhere on deck that they could!

Columbus returned to Spain aboard the *Niña*.

Time to Make a Timer!

How did crewmen aboard the *Niña,* the *Pinta,* or the *Santa Maria* know when it was time to do their chores? They depended on a half-hour sand glass, and the ship's boys who called out the time. "One glass is gone and now the second floweth," the boy on duty would shout. After eight glasses, or four hours, a new boy would come on deck to call out the time. Invite students to make their own sand timers using two plastic soda bottles, salt or sand, masking tape, plastic wrap, and a pin or pen. Have students pour some salt into one of their two bottles, seal the mouth of that bottle by covering it with plastic wrap and attaching the wrap with tape. Then use the pin or pen to puncture a small hole into the plastic wrap. Next, students should firmly tape the mouth of the second bottle over the first one. Students can then turn the bottles over and see how much time it takes for all the salt to run from one bottle into the other. If you like, turn this activity into a "timely" contest by awarding a prize to the child whose sand timer comes closest to measuring exactly 30 seconds or another predetermined amount of time.

What Would You Take On Board?

Personal belongings on Columbus's ships were carried in chests that were about five palms long, three palms wide, and three palms high. (A palm was the measure of length from the thumb to the end of the little finger when the fingers are stretched out.) Have students find or make a box that is approximately this size. Then tell the class to imagine that they are packing as members of Columbus's crew. Ask students to list the items that they would have wanted to take on the voyage. Next, have students estimate whether their belongings would fit in one of these boxes. If not, students will have to cut their lists down even more. Finally, have students share—and compare—their lists with a classmate. What types of items did everyone pack?

Accuracy Not Required

Emphasize to students that many of the measurement tools that Columbus used—from the sand timer and compass to the quadrant and his method of dead reckoning—were imprecise, yet they still helped him to navigate the ocean. Assign a team of students to find out more about each of these tools and/or others. When they're ready, select a spokesperson from each team to explain to the class the tool's purpose, how Columbus used it, and how accurate it tended to be. The group should also be prepared to share the names of tools that are used today to serve the same, or a similar function, and to talk about whether the accuracy of these tools has improved.

The Bookshelf

Nonfiction

- *I, Columbus: My Journal 1492–3* edited by Peter and Connie Roop (Walker and Company, 1990). This book for children is based on the actual log that Columbus kept on his first journey across the Atlantic.

AND DID YOU KNOW . . .

Traditionally, Columbus Day is celebrated on October 12, the day that he and his crew supposedly reached land. But that's the date they reached shore based on the old Julian calendar! If you adjust the date to suit the Gregorian calendar that we use today, Columbus actually landed in the Americas on October 21, 1492.

Fiction

- *Pedro's Journal* by Pam Conrad (Scholastic Inc., 1991). This fictional journal, written from the point of view of a ship's boy aboard the *Santa Maria*, is based on thorough research. Use it as the basis of a discussion about ways Columbus's crew needed to use math.

For Teachers

- *Columbus Day Magic* by James W. Baker (Lerner Publications Co., 1990). Though really designed for young children, this activity book with a Columbus Day theme includes some math activities presented as magic tricks that you can share with your students.

1621
The First Thanksgiving

Key Math Skills Multiplying with fractions
☆ Standard measurement units

What You'll Need A set of the ingredients listed on
the "A Feast Fit for a Pilgrim" worksheet, page 17

Historical Background

Long before there was a Statue of Liberty, people have been coming to America in search of religious and economic freedom. Aboard the *Mayflower,* for example, people who called themselves "Saints" were looking for a way to remain loyal English subjects yet worship in whatever way they chose. William Bradford dubbed others on board "Strangers." These people, consisting mainly of soldiers, servants, and artisans, were primarily interested in reaping economic benefits from the New World.

At first the Saints and the Strangers could hardly wait to reach land and be rid of one another. They soon realized, however, that to endure the harsh conditions of a relatively unsettled area, they would have to stick together. While still on board ship, they wrote up an agreement known as the *Mayflower Compact.*

This document established a "Civil Body Politic," or government, by which everyone agreed to abide. On shore, now united as Pilgrims, they also negotiated a treaty with the local Wampanoag Indians. Indeed, without the cooperation of these Wampanoag neighbors and two other Native American friends—a Patuxet Indian named Squanto, and Chief Samoset of the Pemaquid Indians—the Pilgrims would probably not have survived.

Designed to transport wine, the *Mayflower* could carry 180 tons.

So Where's the Math in That?

When the Pilgrims first came ashore in Plymouth, the season was late autumn. Their food supplies on board ship had diminished, and they had no crops to harvest. Though they were worn out from their long cross-Atlantic journey, they immediately got to work building shelters, hunting, fishing, and gathering foods that grew wild. They also cared for the sick and buried the dead among them.

By the following autumn, things were definitely better. By now Plymouth had a few more homes and shelters. And thanks to the Native Americans, the corn crops were thriving. The settlers decided it was time to celebrate this first harvest with a feast.

The Pilgrims invited Squanto, Samoset, and the Wampanoag chief, Massasoit, to their celebration. Unexpectedly, Massasoit brought about 90 people along!

In this activity, students will adjust some no-cook recipes from colonial America to feed the approximately 140 people who attended that first Thanksgiving. They can then modify the recipes again to feed their own family or class population and/or try to figure out about how much more food the Pilgrims might have served.

AND DID YOU KNOW . . .

Historians are unsure of the actual dates of the first Plymouth Thanksgiving. It was most likely held some time between September 21 and November 9, 1621.

AND DID YOU KNOW . . .

The *Mayflower* had its share of people named Edward, Richard, and Mary. But by far John was the most popular name, shared by 15 of the 50 men on board! William came in second; Edward, third; and the names Richard and Mary tied for fourth place. Among the most unusual names of people on board the *Mayflower*: Oceanus, Resolved, Peregrine, Remember, Humility, Wrestling, and Love.

What to Do

1 Discuss with students the type of preparation that goes into planning a big Thanksgiving dinner, or any type of party. What kinds of things must be thought about in advance? What types of problems can sometimes arise? (In most cases the host or hostess puts together a guest list, plans a menu, and makes sure that there will be enough food and beverages. Problems might include not inviting someone and then having them find out, or having a guest show up who is allergic, or otherwise unable to eat the items being served.)

2 Review with students the story of the first Thanksgiving, as given above. Then ask students what they would do if they were throwing a party and, at the last minute, an extra 90 people showed up! Ask students why they think the Pilgrims did not simply tell Chief Massasoit and his people that there wasn't enough food and that they could not stay.

3 Distribute copies of page 17, "A Feast Fit for a Pilgrim." and tell students that although no one can be sure whether these dishes were served at the first Thanksgiving, they did originate in Colonial America. Working on their own or with a partner, ask students to adjust the recipes so that they would have fed all 140 people at Plymouth's first Thanksgiving feast. If necessary, review how to adjust the recipes, as explained under "What Students Will Learn," on page 14.

4 As a class, go over the worksheet answers. Then, to get an idea how much food this is, have students try to conceptualize about how much space these ingredients might take up. Do students think they would fit in your classroom? A standard refrigerator? How many serving bowls do students estimate would have been needed to serve this amount of food?

Tight Squeeze: Have students figure out how many of their own families' dining tables they'd need to accommodate the approximately 140 people who attended the first Thanksgiving.

5 Point out that many other foods were definitely served at the first Thanksgiving—including fish, duck, deer, goose, corn, carrots, turnips, beets, pumpkins, and onions. After doing additional research, students may wish to put together a plausible menu of items (including amounts!) that might have been served at that three-day Plymouth feast.

6 If you like, ask students to readjust the recipes on the worksheet to feed the number of kids in your classroom, and then work in teams to whip up a sampling of these recipes for a "taste test."

What Students Will Learn

Before they can adjust the recipes on the worksheet, students must first figure out by how much to increase them. For example, if a recipe makes five one-cup servings of Swizzle, and students want 140 servings, they must know to multiply each original ingredient amount by 28 (140 ÷ 5).

As for how to multiply with fractions, there are many tactics that students can choose from. One obvious way is to resort to the standard formula of multiplying numerator times numerator, and denominator times denominator, and then reducing the product. If students have a handle on fractions, however, this is not always necessary. For example, whenever students see a unit fraction—a fraction with a numerator of 1, such as $\frac{1}{2}$, $\frac{1}{3}$, $\frac{1}{4}$, etc.— they can simply divide the other number by the denominator. Students often do this intuitively anyway, such as when they divide a number by 2 to find half ($\frac{1}{2}$) of it.

Similarly, once they know what $\frac{1}{2}$ a number is, they may already be conscious that $\frac{1}{4}$ is exactly $\frac{1}{2}$ of that new number. Suggest to your students that they think of $\frac{1}{4}$ as "quarters," as in quarters of a dollar. As with money, three of them make $\frac{3}{4}$ (three quarters) and six of them are "$1.50"—or one and a half.

AND DID YOU KNOW . . .

The Plymouth harvest festival on which we supposedly base our modern Thanksgiving traditions was not the first day of thanks ever held by settlers in America. A religious celebration offering thanks to God for safe arrival in a settlement called Berkeley Hundred was made by Virginia colonists on December 14, 1619. And even earlier, in 1607, a harvest feast and prayer meeting was held in Maine. Neither of these celebrations was ever repeated, however, because neither of these colonies survived.

WANT TO SIMPLIFY THINGS?

If your students are not yet studying fractions, you can easily adjust these recipes so that they require only whole number multiplication. To do this, multiply each ingredient amount in the "cold slaw" recipe by 2, and each ingredient amount in the Swizzle and Cranberry Conserve recipes by 4 in advance. Note, however, that this will automatically affect the number of servings that each of these recipes makes.

Extensions

What Shall We Measure With?

Point out to students that teaspoons, tablespoons, and measuring cups were probably not common cooking utensils among the early settlers. Speculate with students how the Pilgrims might have measured out ingredients for their recipes instead. Without using standard measurement terms, how else might students describe amounts like one cup, one pound, or one teaspoon? Challenge students to write a paragraph explaining how they could describe one or more of these amounts in terms that a Pilgrim or Native American would understand. (Possible answers include walnut shells, clam shells, or cupped hands.)

Stock Up for Winter!

Tell students that one of the first structures built by the Plymouth colonists was a food storehouse. By late November they tried to have it stocked with enough food to last them until March. Ask students what they would stock away if they had to go shopping in November for enough to last them through the winter. Before they decide, have students estimate about how much food they eat daily, weekly, or monthly. Then, based on these amounts, challenge students to make up their own four-month shopping lists!

Be a Pilgrim Calorie Counter!

In England and Holland, where the Pilgrims had formerly lived, their diet had been largely based on grain, and was thus extremely high in calories. By some estimates, they had once eaten as many as 6,000 calories per person per day. Using a calorie counter, challenge students to estimate about how many calories there might be in a traditional Thanksgiving dinner. (Remind them, however, that the Pilgrims did not eat nearly that much food every day!)

"Corny" Crops

Though many of their other crops failed, the corn that the Pilgrims planted thrived, thanks to the advice provided by Squanto and the other Native Americans. That first winter the Pilgrims calculated that there was enough corn to provide each person with 2 pounds of corn meal per day! Ask students what they would make if they were given 2 pounds of corn meal to cook with daily. Invite students to look through recipe books for ideas, then to share what they find out with the class.

The Bookshelf

Nonfiction

These two selections are filled with more fascinating facts about the Pilgrims, as well as additional recipes from colonial days.

- *Eating the Plates: A Pilgrim Book of Food and Manners* by Lucille Recht Penner (Scholastic, Inc., 1991).

- *Gobble!: The Complete Book of Thanksgiving Words* by Lynda Graham-Barber (Avon Books, 1993.)

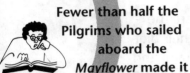

AND DID YOU KNOW . . . Fewer than half the Pilgrims who sailed aboard the *Mayflower* made it through that first rough winter in Plymouth. At their harvest festival the following autumn, Native Americans actually outnumbered colonists about 2 to 1!

Fiction

- *Constance: A Story of Early Plymouth* by Patricia Clapp (Beech Street Books, 1968). This fictional account of a girl's coming of age in Plymouth colony, written in a journal format, is based on actual historic information. As they read, students can create their own timelines recounting the settling of Plymouth, Massachusetts. Then, using library resources, they can expand their timelines with additional facts.

- *Three Young Pilgrims* by Cheryl Harness (Bradbury Press, 1992). Like *Constance*, this picture book is also based on the story of an actual Pilgrim family. Though catalogued as fiction, this small, pretty volume also includes kid-friendly, yet accurate, timelines, maps, and illustrations of the Pilgrim voyage, the ship they sailed on, and the area they settled.

For Teachers

- *Pilgrims* by Susan Moger (Scholastic Professional Books, 1995). Though geared primarily toward teachers of children in grades K to 3, many of this book's activities (including some math activities!), developed in cooperation with Pilgrim Hall Museum, can easily be adapted to suit the needs of older students.

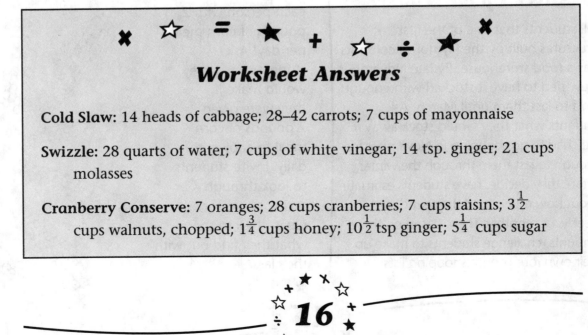

Worksheet Answers

Cold Slaw: 14 heads of cabbage; 28–42 carrots; 7 cups of mayonnaise

Swizzle: 28 quarts of water; 7 cups of white vinegar; 14 tsp. ginger; 21 cups molasses

Cranberry Conserve: 7 oranges; 28 cups cranberries; 7 cups raisins; $3\frac{1}{2}$ cups walnuts, chopped; $1\frac{3}{4}$ cups honey; $10\frac{1}{2}$ tsp ginger; $5\frac{1}{4}$ cups sugar

Name_____

A Feast Fit for a Pilgrim

*H*ere are some "no-cook" recipes that were actually made in Pilgrim days. Try adjusting them to feed everyone at the Plymouth Thanksgiving feast!

Swizzle
(a cool, sweet beverage)

To make 5 one-cup servings:

1 quart, water

¼ cup white vinegar

½ teaspoon ginger

¾ cup molasses

To make 140 one-cup servings:

_____ quarts, water

_____ cups white vinegar

_____ teaspoons ginger

_____ cups molasses

Mix the ingredients in a glass jar, and shake well.
Refrigerate overnight and serve cold.

Cold Slaw
(or "cole slaw," as it is commonly called today)

To make 10 half-cup servings:

1 small head of cabbage

2–3 carrots

½ cup mayonnaise

To make 140 half-cup servings:

_____ small heads of cabbage

_____ carrots

_____ cups of mayonnaise

plus . . . a dash of lemon juice or vinegar, salt, pepper, and a pinch of sugar

Grate the cabbage and carrots and mix them with the mayonnaise.
Season to taste.

Cranberry Conserve
(or jam)

To make about 20 quarter-cup servings:

1 large orange

4 cups fresh cranberries, washed

1 cup golden raisins

½ cup walnuts, chopped

¼ cup honey

1½ teaspoons ginger

¾ cup sugar

To make about 140 quarter-cup servings:

_____ oranges

_____ cups fresh cranberries

_____ cups golden raisins

_____ cups walnuts, chopped

_____ cups honey

_____ teaspoons ginger

_____ cups sugar

Wash the orange and cut it into quarters. Remove the seeds.

Chop the orange(s) and cranberries, either in a food processor or by hand.

Mix the chopped fruit with the raisins, walnuts, honey, ginger, and sugar.

Chill for at least 4 hours and then spread on bread or serve by itself.

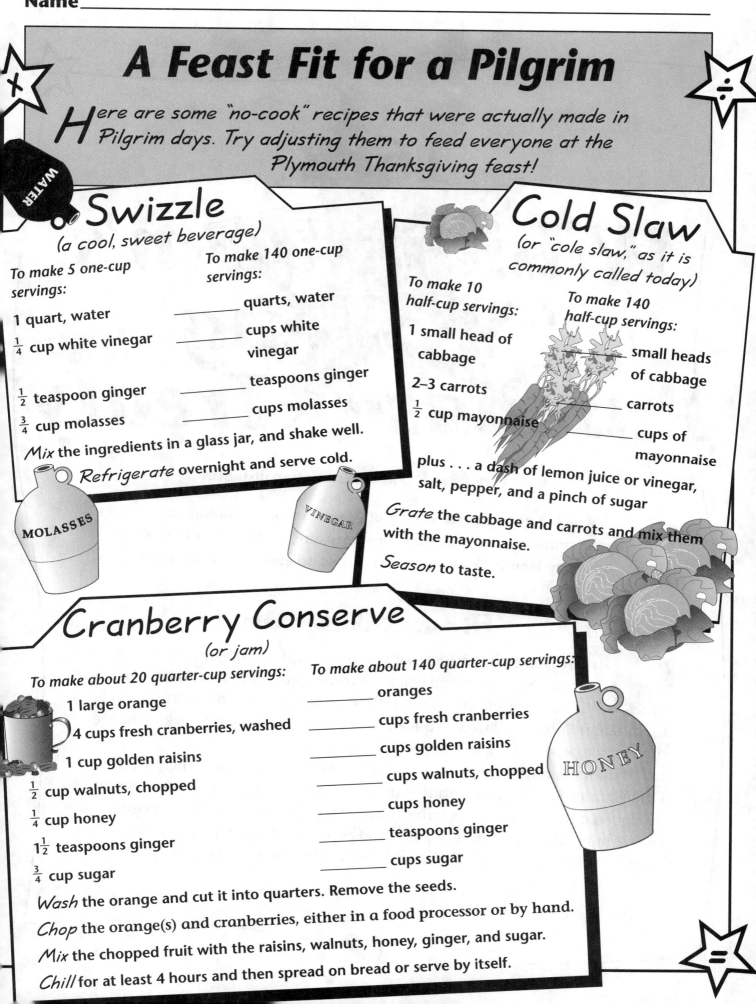

1682
William Penn's "Walking Purchase" Treaty

Key Math Skill Estimating distances

What You'll Need A map of Pennsylvania ☆ A map of your own area (optional) ☆ A yardstick, tape measure, and/or other tools that measure length ☆ Pushpins or crayons, to mark points on a map

Historical Background

Throughout the fifteenth, sixteenth, and seventeenth centuries, European explorers and colonists continued to arrive in North America. Different groups often stuck different flags in the ground, claiming land for different European kings or queens. Very few were willing to acknowledge that native peoples had any right to this land.

William Penn, however, was not like these others. In 1682, the year after King Charles II of England granted him the area now known as Pennsylvania, he signed a treaty with the nearby Native Americans. As a Quaker, Penn did not believe in fighting. Having been jailed and persecuted back in England for his own religious beliefs, Penn was even more determined to prove that people of differing faiths could get along.

So Where's the Math in That?

The agreement that William Penn and Chief Lapowinsa of the Delaware Indians signed in 1682 is known as the "Walking Purchase" treaty. During the meeting, which is thought to have been held a little north of what is now downtown Philadelphia, the Indians agreed to sell Penn some land in eastern Pennsylvania between the Lehigh River and the Delaware River. The Native Americans did not rely on units such as miles or meters to measure distance. So, by the terms of the agreement, the colonists were allowed to take as much land as they could walk in three days.

William Penn met the chiefs of the Delaware tribes at Shakamaxon (now part of Philadelphia).

In this activity, students will figure out about how much land they think Penn's followers were entitled to, based on the terms of the agreement. They will then compare their results with the amount of land that Penn and his descendants eventually got.

What to Do

1 Share with students the history of William Penn and Pennsylvania, as given above. Then display a large map of Pennsylvania, and ask students to locate the point where the Lehigh and Delaware Rivers meet, not far from the present-day cities of Allentown and Bethlehem. Explain that, by the terms of the "Walking Purchase" treaty, the colonists were entitled to as much land north of this point, right along the Delaware River, as a person could walk in three days.

The Delaware River, Pennsylvania's eastern border, separates the Keystone State from New York and New Jersey. The Lehigh meets the Delaware east of Bethlehem.

2 Organize students into cooperative groups of three or four students each, and have each group estimate about how many miles' worth of land they believe Penn and his people should have taken. Students should note that the treaty didn't specify how quickly the person could walk in the three days, or how much time they might allot for eating or sleeping. Each group of students will have to decide these things for itself.

3 Brainstorm with students some of the methods they might use to figure out how far a person could walk in three days. (For ideas, see "Ways to Estimate 'Walking Distance'" on page 21.) Then leave it up to each group of students to decide for themselves which method to use.

4 When each group has agreed on a distance, have students figure out how far north along the Delaware River that would be. Then have each group use a different color crayon to mark this spot on a large map.

5 Offer group members a chance to share their results with the rest of the students. Each group should explain the distance and location they came up with as well as how they arrived at their estimate. Discuss possible reasons for any discrepancies.

6 By now, students may be curious to know how much land William Penn and his descendants really did get from the Delaware Indians. Share with them the following facts:

Even though Penn was entitled to settle three days' worth of land, he decided to settle only one and a half days' worth of land first. He calculated that amount to be about 40 miles. Relations between the colonists and the Indians were fine for almost 70 years. When Penn died, the governorship of the colony passed first to his wife, and then to his two sons. In 1737, Thomas Penn decided it was time to claim the remaining day and a half's worth of land. He offered a reward to the person who could travel farthest in that time period. The winner, Edward Marshall, traveled $66\frac{1}{2}$ miles in 36 hours. (Many say that he ran much of the way.)

7 Ask students to figure out the total number of miles of land Penn and his ancestors ended up taking from the Indians. (40 miles + $66\frac{1}{2}$ miles equal $106\frac{1}{2}$ miles.) Next have students use a map to figure out about how far up the Delaware River this would take them, as compared with the estimates that they arrived at on their own.

AND DID YOU KNOW . . .

By the late 1760s, only about a thousand Indians were left in Pennsylvania, and many of these had been pushed farther and farther west. Others had moved to Ohio. Because they felt they had been so mistreated by the English settlers, many Native Americans chose to side with France during the French and Indian War.

AND DID YOU KNOW . . .

The Liberty Bell came to Philadelphia from England in 1752. It had been designed to mark the 50th anniversary of William Penn's Charter of Privileges, a precursor of later documents, such as the Universal Declaration of Human Rights.

What Students Will Learn

In this activity, students will find out that measurement is not always an "exact science." By using different techniques to estimate the same distance, and then using scale to find these distances on a map, students will explore some reasons why discrepancies among measurements can easily exist.

Extensions

Map Out the City

Share with students this 1682 description of Philadelphia, as given by Thomas Holme, one of the city's original surveyors:

In the center of the city is a square of ten acres, at each angle are to be houses for publick affairs, as a Meeting House, Assembly or State House, Market House, School House, and several other buildings for public concerns. There is also in each quarter of ye city a square of eight acres to be for the like uses as the Moorfields in London, and eight streets beside the High street that runs from front to front, and twenty streets besides the Broad street that runs across the city from side to side; all these streets are fifty foot in breadth.

Based on this description, challenge students to use graph paper to draw a picture showing how they imagine the city was laid out. They can then compare these drawings with actual maps of Philadelphia, either as it looks today or as it looked back in the 1700s. A simple map of the original layout, drawn by Penn himself, can be found in numerous sources, including *Colonial Histories: Pennsylvania* and *Makers of American History (1536–1800)*, both of which are listed in the "The Bookshelf" on page 22. Students may also enjoy describing the layout of their own home or neighborhood in a paragraph, and then challenging a classmate to draw a map of that area, based on the description. The exercise will teach them how difficult it is both to describe a site accurately and to convert a verbal description into a precise visual plan.

Take a "State Stroll"

Invite students to look up the distance from end-to-end of Pennsylvania, or the distance around Pennsylvania's perimeter. Then ask them to figure out about how many "days' worth" of time it would have taken to purchase this amount of land, using the "Walking Purchase" approach. Students may also enjoy figuring out the amount of time it would take to "purchase" their own town, city, or state in walking distance. Or, challenge students to figure out the "most expensive" and "least expensive" states in terms of how long these places would take to walk.

WAYS TO ESTIMATE "WALKING DISTANCE"

Here are some methods students may wish to use to calculate about how far they could walk in three days:

◆ For five minutes, students can walk back and forth, from end to end of their classroom, measure that distance, and then figure out how many five minutes there are in 72 hours (three days).

◆ Students who walk to school may want to figure out the distance from their house to the school building, perhaps by asking a parent to drive them, so that they can clock the distance on the car's odometer. Students can then use this mileage data, and their knowledge of about how long the walk takes, to figure out how far they could walk in three days.

◆ Another method might be to figure out the distance in a "footstep," decide about how many footsteps a person can take in a certain amount of time, such as a minute, and then work from there.

Design a Hex

To spark growth within his young settlement, Thomas Penn encouraged people to relocate to his colony. He even posted advertisements throughout Europe to that effect. Among those who took him up on the offer were many Amish and Mennonite people. Like the Quakers, the members of these Protestant religious groups, descendants of the Anabaptists, were being persecuted in Europe for their religious beliefs. Today, the descendants of these "Pennsylvania Germans" are still known for their beautiful folk art, especially the hex signs that decorate their barns, housewares, and furniture. (Samples of these designs are shown here.) After sharing some of these designs with students, invite them to research the meaning behind the geometric patterns. Then distribute a compass, ruler, and crayons, and allow students to create some hex designs of their own.

Six-pointed star: a harbinger of love or of a good marriage.

Eight-pointed star: a sign of good will.

Double five-pointed star: a sign of sun or good weather.

The Bookshelf

Nonfiction

- *Kids' America* by Steven Caney (Workman Publishing, 1978). This big activity book of Americana includes lots of information about early American hobbies, games, and crafts. Included is both background information about, and directions on how to create, hex designs.

Fiction

- *Weasel* by Cynthia DeFelice (Macmillan Publishing Co., 1990). Though set in Ohio about 100 years after Thomas Penn wronged the Delaware Indians, this book tells the story of a white boy who learns first-hand of the legacy of the Europeans' mistreatment of the Native Americans.

For Teachers

These two books provide further information, and maps, related to William Penn's original settlement.

- *Colonial Histories: Pennsylvania* by Lucille Wallower (Thomas Nelson & Sons, 1967).

- *Makers of American History (1536–1800)* (Encyclopedia Britannica Educational Corp., 1971).

AND DID YOU KNOW . . .

Penn chose the name *Philadelphia* for the city that he hoped would become a haven of religious freedom. In Greek, it means "Brotherly Love." He did not, however, want to name his colony Pennsylvania. He thought of calling it either New Wales, or simply Sylvania (which means "woods"). Out of modesty, he did not think it was appropriate to give the place his family's name. Obviously, however, the king of England disagreed.

AND DID YOU KNOW . . .

The "Pennsylvania Dutch" who live in Pennsylvania today are really the Amish and Mennonite descendants of the Pennsylvania Germans. They're called "Dutch" because, over time, the German word for "German," which is *Deutsch*, came to be pronounced in English as "Dutch."

1750–1769

Ben Franklin's Magic Squares

Key Math Skills Guess and check
☆ Whole number addition and subtraction

What You'll Need Calculators

Historical Background

By **the age of 46,** Ben Franklin had already had more careers than most people have in a lifetime. He was the official printer for the colony of Pennsylvania, he published his own newspaper and *Poor Richard's Almanack,* and he served as deputy postmaster of Philadelphia. He had also helped organize Philadelphia's first volunteer fire brigade and the first lending library in America. In 1742, at the age of 36, Franklin invented the Franklin Stove, which heated a room better than any other in the colonies and also used less wood than most others. Yet Franklin's years of productivity were just beginning. Ben Franklin would continue to make outstanding contributions to society until his death, at the then extraordinarily ripe age of 84, in 1790.

The year 1752 was no exception. That year, Franklin conducted his famous experiment with electricity, using a kite, wire, silk ribbon, and a small key. Less publicized, and admittedly less earth-shattering, were Franklin's "magic squares," which he had begun "experimenting" with while a clerk of the Pennsylvania Colonial Assembly. Although Franklin readily conceded that he could think of no practical use for these squares, he still enjoyed creating them. He considered the one shown on page 30 to be "the most magically magical of any magic square ever made by any magician."

So Where's the Math in That?

Your students may think that typing a paper without spelling mistakes is almost impossible, even with the help of today's technology. But back in Franklin's time, the printing process was even more tedious than using a manual typewriter is today! Every letter, space bar, and punctuation symbol had to be picked individually out of a large tray called a type case. It then had to be arranged, symbol by symbol, onto a metal rod known as a "composing stick." Opportunities for errors abounded. So it is not very surprising that this magic square, of which Franklin was so proud, was often reprinted incorrectly. The version shown on page 30 is no exception. It contains errors that may have first been published in 1769. The trick is to find the errors.

Proud of his magic squares, Franklin was able to dash them off.

What to Do

1 As a warm-up exercise, challenge students to arrange the numbers 1 to 9 on a three-by-three grid so that each row, column, and diagonal of numbers add up to the same "magic" total. (You might give them a hint that the numbers add up to 15.) If it's done properly, students should arrive at a configuration similar to this:

8	1	6
3	5	7
4	9	2

This type of number arrangement, tell students, is known as a "magic square."

2 Share with students the "Historical Background" about Ben Franklin and explain that, as a young man, he had a habit of creating magic squares for enjoyment. Unfortunately, because his squares were large and contained so many digits, they could easily be copied incorrectly. That's exactly what happened to the square that students are about to see.

3 Organize students into cooperative learning groups, and distribute a copy of "Ben Franklin's Magic Square," on page 30, to each child. Explain to students that, aside from being larger, this square differs in at least one other way from the simple three-by-three grids that they just made. As with the squares that they created, each row and column should still amount to the same "magic" total. But rather than the diagonals, the "bent rows," or V-shapes, that are indicated should also equal this magic sum.

4 Explain to students that three numbers between 1 and 256 were mistakenly repeated on this particular magic square, and three others were omitted by accident. Working with their groups, have students first identify the three numbers that appear on the square twice, as well as the three that are missing. As a group, they should then work together to determine the correct box in which each missing number belongs.

What Students Will Learn

Although this activity is a challenging one, students will find that it should not be at all overwhelming if they approach it systematically. For example, one logical way to get started would be to first figure out the "magic sum" of each row and column. (This will require finding the sum of at least two different columns or rows.) Students might also assign each group member the job of searching a certain subset of numbers for the repeated digits—as well as for the ones that are missing. They can then test each missing number in a space where a duplicated number appears. Students should keep track of which numbers they've tried in each space, so that they don't waste time repeating their work.

Setting a magic square by hand was no easy task for early printers.

Extensions

Check Up on Ben!

In a letter to a friend in London, Peter Collinson, Ben Franklin boasted that his "magical" magic square contained these properties:

- Every straight row (horizontal or vertical) of 16 numbers added together makes 2,056, and half of each row makes half of 2,056 (1,028).

- The bent row of 16 numbers ascending diagonally and descending diagonally, *viz.*, from 64 ascending to 52, and from 77 descending to 65 and every one of its parallel bent rows of 16 numbers make 2,056.

- The four corner numbers with the four middle numbers make 2,056.

- If you cut a square hole in a piece of paper of such a size as to show through it just 16 of the little squares when laid on the greater square, the sum of the 16 numbers appearing through the hole, wherever it is placed on the greater square, should equal 2,056.

When students are convinced that they have accurately corrected the square, present them with these properties as a self-checking device. Or, if you prefer (especially if you work with advanced students), challenge them to find some of these properties of the square on their own.

A Quick Flash of Math

In his famous kite experiment of 1752, Ben Franklin tested his theory that lightning was a form of electricity. Today we know that he was right. We also know that the light from a lightning flash travels at about 186,282 miles per second. The thunder that follows it, by comparison, can only travel about $\frac{1}{4}$ mile per second. (That's because light travels much faster than sound.) So if you hear thunder four seconds after you see lightning, tell students, the lightning is about one mile away. To help kids understand this concept, ask two volunteers to stand next to each other in front of the classroom. Explain to the class that one of these students represents "lightning," and the other represents "thunder." Then have "lightning" quickly cross to the other side of the room. When that child stops, tell students that the lightning has "struck." Now have "thunder" walk slowly toward "lightning." Each time "thunder" takes a step, you should explain that it has gone $\frac{1}{4}$ mile, and has traveled for 1 second. Add up the seconds—and the quarter miles—it takes "thunder" to reach "lightning." Then reduce the fraction. That's about how far away the lightning was. When students grasp the idea, quiz them with questions like these: About how far away is a bolt of lightning if you hear thunder after eight seconds? (2 miles) two seconds? ($\frac{1}{2}$ mile) 10 seconds? ($2\frac{1}{2}$ miles) 20 seconds? (5 miles). Students may also enjoy making up problems similar to these on their own.

An Almanac Scavenger Hunt

If a current edition of either *Poor Richard's Almanack* or *The Farmer's Almanac* is available to your students, challenge them to look up facts about tides, the weather, etc. for your area, and for this particular season. If you like, turn the activity into an almanac "Scavenger Hunt," in which teams are challenged to create the largest list of almanac facts about your region of the country this month.

Worksheet Answers

The printers made three errors.

- In column 1, row 8, "55" should be "53."

- In column 7, row 10, "241" should be "211."

- In column 14, row 14, "90" should be "99."

200	217	232	249	8	25	40	57	72	89	104	121	136	153	168	185
58	39	26	7	250	231	218	199	186	167	154	135	122	103	90	71
198	219	230	251	6	27	38	59	70	91	102	123	134	155	166	187
60	37	28	5	252	229	220	197	188	165	156	133	124	101	92	69
201	216	233	248	9	24	41	56	73	88	105	120	137	152	169	184
55	42	23	10	247	234	215	202	183	170	151	138	119	106	87	74
203	214	235	246	11	22	43	54	75	86	107	118	139	150	171	182
53	44	21	12	245	236	213	204	181	172	149	140	117	108	85	76
205	212	237	244	13	20	45	52	77	84	109	116	141	148	173	180
51	46	19	14	243	238	211	206	179	174	147	142	115	110	83	78
207	210	239	242	15	18	47	50	79	82	111	114	143	146	175	178
49	48	17	16	241	240	209	208	177	176	145	144	113	112	81	80
196	221	228	253	4	29	36	61	68	93	100	125	132	157	164	189
62	35	30	3	254	227	222	195	190	163	158	121	126	99	94	67
194	223	226	255	2	31	34	63	66	95	98	127	130	159	162	191
64	33	32	1	256	225	224	193	192	161	160	129	128	97	96	65

Do-it-Yourself Magic

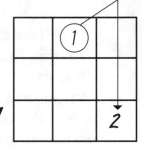

Post the steps below so that students can learn to create their own large magic squares. Then, after having students experiment with them for a while, hold a discussion about the ways that these squares differ from the one of which Franklin was so proud.

To Make a Magic Square with an Odd Number of Boxes

- Start with a square that has an uneven number of cells in each row and column.
- Place any number in the center square of the top row.
- Using numbers that grow consecutively larger or smaller, place each remaining number in the box that is one higher, and directly to the right, of the one before it. When this is not possible, use whichever one of the three following directions applies:

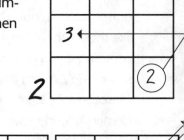

1 If moving above and to the right puts you on *top* of the square, go to the bottom of that column.

2 If moving above and to the right puts you to the *right* of the square, go to the far left of that row.

3 If moving above and to the right puts you in an already occupied cell, or puts you both on top *and* to the right of the square, put the next number directly below the previous one.

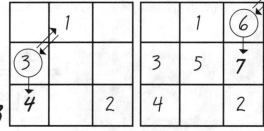

To Make a Magic Square with an Even Number of Boxes

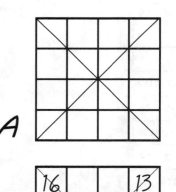

A Start with a square that has a multiple of four cells in each row and column. (i.e., 4, 8, 12, etc.) Draw the two diagonals lightly in pencil, as shown.

B Start with the last number that you expect your square to contain. (i.e., for a 4 x 4 square, that number might be 16.) Place this number in the cell that is in the upper left-hand corner of your square.

Counting backward, and working across each row of the square from left to right, place the appropriate number in each cell that has a pencil mark in it. For example, in a 4 x 4 square that will contain the numbers 1 to 16, your square should now look like the one at left (B).

C Now start at the top and count "forward," filling in any blank cells that are still remaining. When you're done, your magic square is complete!

The Bookshelf

Nonfiction

- *The Many Lives of Benjamin Franklin* by Mary Pope Osborne (Dial Books for Young Readers, 1990). In this thorough book for more advanced readers, students will find a photograph of an 18th century type case (which holds the letters for a printing press), and a diagram showing how the Franklin stove worked. The book concludes with a comprehensive list of Ben Franklin's "famous firsts" and his other accomplishments.

- *A Book About Benjamin Franklin* by Ruth Belov Gross (Scholastic Inc., 1975). An easy read for fifth graders, this book ends with a simple math experiment that students can try, which Franklin made only about a year before he died.

- *Benjamin Franklin: Scientist and Inventor* by Eve B. Feldman (Franklin Watts, 1990). This book focuses on Franklin's accomplishments as a scientist, rather than as a statesman. Kids with scientific minds will be fascinated.

AND DID YOU KNOW . . . Franklin was the only person who had a hand in drafting, negotiating, and signing all four major documents crucial to establishing the new nation: the Declaration of Independence, the Treaty of Alliance with France, the Treaty of Peace with Great Britain, and the Constitution of the United States.

- *Arithmetricks* by Jerome S. Meyer (Scholastic, Inc., 1974). Among other "math magic" that students will find in this book are more fun facts about magic squares and the amazing properties that they contain.

Fiction

- *Ben and Me* by Robert Lawson (Little Brown and Company, 1939). This fictional account of Ben Franklin's life is told from the point of view of Amos, a mouse that insists that the world has him to thank for Ben Franklin's many accomplishments. One way to extend this story would be to have students write a new chapter from Amos's point of view, in which Amos helps Franklin improve in math or complete his phenomenal magic square.

For Teachers

- "Benjamin Franklin's 'Magical Square of 16,'" by Albert Chandler (*Journal of The Franklin Institute*, April 1951 issue). Though it may take some digging to find, this thorough article about Franklin's famous magic square is well worth the trouble for those who find themselves extremely fascinated by the topic.

- "A Reexamination of the Franklin Square," by Charles J. Jacobs (*The Mathematics Teacher*, January 1971 issue). This article, which is only recommended for those completely taken with the exploration of magic squares, explains how readers can create their own magic squares similar to the ones that Franklin once made.

Ben Franklin's Magic Square

When you hear the name Ben Franklin, you may think of Poor Richard's Almanack, the invention of bifocals, or the signing of the Declaration of Independence and the Constitution. But Franklin had another talent that is not often mentioned. He was a whiz at creating magic squares! In this original "Franklin square," each row, column, and "bent-row" (V-shape of numbers) should add up to the same total. They don't, however, because of a printing error that occurred when the square was published back in 1769.

To fix the square, find the three numbers between 1 and 256 that are repeated, and the three numbers that were left out by accident. Can you figure out in which box each of these missing numbers belongs?

200	217	232	249	8	25	40	57	72	89	104	121	136	153	168	185
58	39	26	7	250	231	218	199	186	167	154	135	122	103	90	71
198	219	230	251	6	27	38	59	70	91	102	123	134	155	166	187
60	37	28	5	252	229	220	197	188	165	156	133	124	101	92	69
201	216	233	248	9	24	41	56	73	88	105	120	137	152	169	184
55	42	23	10	247	204	215	202	183	170	151	138	119	106	87	74
203	214	265	246	11	22	43	54	75	86	107	118	139	150	171	182
53	44	21	12	245	236	213	204	181	172	149	140	117	108	85	76
265	212	267	244	13	20	45	52	77	84	109	116	141	148	173	180
51	46	19	14	243	288	241	206	179	174	147	142	115	110	83	78
207	210	239	242	15	18	47	50	79	82	111	114	143	146	175	198
49	48	17	16	241	240	209	208	177	176	145	144	113	112	81	80
186	221	228	253	4	29	36	61	68	93	100	125	132	157	164	189
62	35	30	3	254	227	222	195	190	163	158	131	126	90	94	67
194	223	226	255	2	31	34	63	66	95	98	127	130	159	162	191
64	33	32	1	256	225	224	193	192	161	160	129	128	97	96	65

1787-1788
The U.S. Constitution Takes Shape

Key Math Skills   Division with remainders ☆ Rounding decimals

What You'll Need   A chart showing the "population"
(total class size) of every class or grade in your school ☆ Calculators

Historical Background

Despite their differences, the American colonists were unified enough to fight, and defeat, the British in the American Revolution. But after the war ended, it became clear that most of these same people felt greater allegiance toward their home states than they did toward the country as a whole. A weak federal government was formed, but it did not have the authority to enforce laws, establish a national monetary system, or collect federal taxes. The Founding Fathers realized that this was not good enough. But what should they do? To resolve the problem, 55 delegates from the 13 colonies met in Philadelphia, Pennsylvania, in the summer of 1787. After a good deal of debate, argument, and compromise, the Constitution of the United States was ratified and signed. This Constitution established the government that we still have in the United States today.

So Where's the Math in That?

One particularly thorny issue for the delegates at the Constitutional Convention was trying to determine whether all of the states should be treated equally in the new government (that is, whether each state was entitled to one vote), or whether those that were larger and had more people were entitled to have "a louder say." Finally everyone agreed to organize a Congress made up of two "houses," or parts. In the Senate, each state would be equally represented by two senators. But in the House of Representatives, representation would be based on population. The more people living in a particular state, the more representatives that state would be allotted. As your students will discover in a simplified simulation of the process, even this "fair" way of determining representation is not as simple—or as "fair"—as it at first sounds.

What to Do

1 Offer students a brief summary of the problems faced by the delegates to the Constitutional Convention, as described above.

2 Tell students that in order to better appreciate the problems that the delegates faced, they are to imagine that each class in the school represents a different state in a newly formed government. Delegates from this government have recently met and have agreed to create a Congress similar to the one that exists in the United States today. Each "state" in this new nation will be allowed to send two senators to the Congress. They will also be able to send a number of representatives that reflect the relative population of their "class state."

3 On the chalkboard, post a chart that shows the "population" (the total class size) of each class (or each grade) in your school building. The chart should look something like the one to the left.

Class	Class Size
Kindergarten	27
First Grade	31
Second Grade	26
Third Grade (A)	30
Third Grade (B)	28
Fourth Grade	31
Fifth Grade	27
TOTAL:	200

4 Based on their chart, ask students to first determine how many senators will be elected to their new Congress. (Since each class can elect two senators, the total number of senators will be double the number of classes—or "states"—that exist in the school.)

5 Next, tell students that they will be allowed to appoint one representative to the House of Representatives for every 10 kids in the school's total population. Thus, in the sample school government shown above, 20 representatives would be appointed. (Obviously, this sample is simplified by the fact that the total population is a round number. In most cases, however, students will have to decide whether they want to round this figure up or down.)

6 Explain to students that, in the United States, each state is entitled to at least one representative—even if its population is very small. To make sure that everyone in your school government also gets at least one representative, tell students that you are going to start by allotting them that one representative immediately. After doing so, your chart will then look something like this:

Class	Class Size	Representatives
Kindergarten	27	1
First Grade	31	1
Second Grade	26	1
Third Grade (A)	30	1
Third Grade (B)	28	1
Fourth Grade	31	1
Fifth Grade	27	1
TOTAL:	200	7
Number left to assign:		13

7 Now comes the trickiest part of all. Tell students that they must figure out how to allot the remaining representatives among all of the "states" in their government. One seemingly fair way to do it, for example, would be to divide the number of remaining representatives (13) equally into each class state's

total population. When we do this, however, we wind up with long, unwieldy decimal fractions, like the ones in the last column on this chart.

Class	Class Size	Representatives	Dividing the Remaining Reps Equally
Kindergarten	27	1	2.076923
First Grade	31	1	2.3846153
Second Grade	26	1	2.0
Third Grade (A)	30	1	2.3076923
Third Grade (B)	28	1	2.1538461
Fourth Grade	31	1	2.3846153
Fifth Grade	27	1	2.076923
TOTAL:	200	7	

8 Of course, we could always simplify these numbers by rounding. But if we do that we wind up with a total of 21 representatives, rather than the 20 that our "constitution" calls for. One class state will have to lose a representative; in this sample case that will probably be the second grade, since it has the smallest population of any in our government.

9 Hold a class discussion about whether this method of deciding representation seems fair. (Obviously, results in your own version of this simulation will differ, depending on class size, and your school's total population. In each case, however, similar mathematical difficulties should arise with which students will have to contend.)

What Students Will Learn

In addition to gaining a basic understanding of the workings of the United States government, students will also learn some real-life applications for whole number division. They will contend with the issue of what a decimal fraction represents, and what must be considered when deciding whether to round it up or down to the nearest whole number. Basically, they will experiment with various ways to deal with numbers that can not be split into perfectly even parts.

AND DID YOU KNOW . . .
Only once since 1911 have there been more than 435 representatives in the House of Representatives. In 1959 that number was temporarily increased to 437 when Alaska and Hawaii were admitted as states.

Extensions

Figure Out What Fair Is

Working in small groups, encourage students to come up with their own definitions of "fairness." Then have them make a list of the ways in which the current method of choosing representatives (as they understand it from the simulation) does—or does not—seem fair. If students think that this is a fair way to decide on representation, ask them how they would feel if they belonged to a class or state that had to give up a vote because of the rounding process. If students think this method unfair, challenge them to suggest a more equitable alternative. If you wish, use this topic as the focus of a class debate.

Keep the Government Alive!

Now that kids have a general idea of how at least one branch of the Federal government works, invite them to continue the scenario. This might entail having students actually vote for a school president and a Congress. The president can then appoint a nine-member Supreme Court, to be confirmed by a majority vote in the Senate. As a next step, offer

members of this new student government a series of issues of consequence to deal with, such as what kinds of "laws" should be established to deal with disagreements among students, how the government should go about raising money, and what kinds of dealings the school should have with other schools in the area. Remind students that, as in the United States, any decisions made by the president must also be approved by a majority in Congress. The president also has the power to veto laws agreed on in Congress, and the Supreme Court has the right to question whether these decisions and laws agree with the Constitution.

Are There Any Fractions in the House?

Point out to students that before the Constitution was able to go into effect, nine states—or $\frac{2}{3}$ of the total 13 states— had to approve it. Today the fraction $\frac{2}{3}$ is still an important one in our government. For example, even if the President vetoes a bill (or suggested law), it can still become a law if $\frac{2}{3}$ of both the Senate and the House of Representatives vote for it. A new amendment to the Constitution also requires a $\frac{2}{3}$ vote by both houses of Congress, or $\frac{2}{3}$ of all state

AND DID YOU KNOW . . . Representatives have always been elected by the people. But until the passage of the 17th Amendment in 1913, senators were selected by each state's legislature.

legislatures can request that a national convention be held to consider a new amendment. To become part of the Constitution, however, a different fraction also becomes crucial: $\frac{3}{4}$ of all state legislatures must also support a constitutional amendment. Using these facts, invite students to figure out exactly how many senators and representatives have been needed to approve a bill, both today and in history. (For example, when the nation was first founded, there were 65 representatives in Congress. Two thirds of that number is 43 representatives. In 1911, Congress set the maximum number of representatives at 435. Two thirds of that number is 290. The number of senators is always equal to two times the number of states in the Union.)

The Bookshelf

Nonfiction

- *Shh! We're Writing the Constitution* by Jean Fritz (Scholastic, 1987). Fritz is a master at telling history like a story—and a comical, enjoyable one at that. This book is no different. Kids will meet the "characters" who attended the Constitutional Convention.

- *Our Congress* by Michael Weber (The Millbrook Press, 1994). This easy-to-read and up-to-date explanation of Congress describes the functions of both the Senate and the House of Representatives, and then walks students through the passage of a particular bill.

Fiction

- *Jump Ship to Freedom* by James Lincoln Collier and Christopher Collier (Delacorte Press, 1981). In this story, a 14-year-old slave, hoping to use his late father's soldiers' notes to buy his and his mother's freedom, winds up at the Constitutional Convention in Philadelphia.

- *Mr. Smith Goes to Washington* (1939 film, directed by Frank Capra). Students may enjoy this fictionalized (and idealized) account of how the Senate works.

For Teachers

- *Counting for Representation: The Census and the Constitution*, an eight-page brochure from the Census Bureau, goes into detail about the history, as well as the math involved, in apportioning representatives among the states. (For sale by Customer Services [DUSD], Bureau of the Census, Washington, DC 20233. Price: 50¢ per copy for two-color brochure; 25¢ per copy for reproducibles.)

AND DID YOU KNOW . . . At the time of the Constitutional Convention, N Jersey was one the "small" states that fea that the large states wou control the Congress. Ironi due to its large urban population, New Jersey is longer very small—popula wise, anyway. Today Ne Jersey has more votes in House of Representativ than Alaska, Delaware Hawaii, Idaho, Maine, Nevada, North Dakota Rhode Island, Utah, and Wyoming combined.

1814 Star-Spangled Banners

Key Math Skill   Symmetry

What You'll Need   Rulers ☆ Scissors
☆ Red, white, and blue construction paper
☆ One or more U.S. flags—preferably of different sizes
☆ A hand mirror (optional)   ☆ A calculator (optional)

Historical Background

Just months before the end of the War of 1812, an American lawyer named Francis Scott Key found himself a prisoner on board a British ship in the Chesapeake Bay, not far from Baltimore, MD. As he watched from the ship, British forces launched an attack on America's Fort McHenry. All night long, Key wondered and worried whether "by the dawn's early light," the Stars and Stripes would still be flying. When he saw that they were, he was inspired to write "The Defence of Fort McHenry," the poem that, renamed "The Star-Spangled Banner," later became the words of the U.S. national anthem.

Fifteen stars and 15 stripes decorated the flag that Key saw waving over Fort McHenry. The design had been adopted by the United States almost 20 years

earlier, in 1795. Yet, by 1814, there were already 18 states in the Union. Congress did not decide until 1818 that one star should adorn the flag for each state in the Union. And, believe it or not, it wasn't until 1912—the year that Arizona and New Mexico entered the Union—that a law went into effect describing exactly how those stars were to be arranged.

So Where's the Math in That?

On June 14, 1777, Congress passed a resolution declaring that "the flag of the 13 United States be 13 stripes, alternate red and white; that the union be 13 stars, white in a blue field, representing a new constellation." Notice that this resolution didn't specify exactly how these stars were to be arranged. In his decree of 1912, President William Howard Taft chose to arrange the stars on the United States flag in rows, horizontally. But, as the samples on the "Stars and Symmetry Forever" worksheet (page 43) show, there were numerous other possibilities from which he could have chosen—all of which had been used at one time or another in United States history.

In this activity, students will identify all of the symmetrical star arrangements that they can find on the worksheet. They will then experiment to see how many other symmetrical ways they can find to arrange 13 five-pointed stars.

What to Do

1 Ask students for a definition of symmetry. Then invite them to look around the room, and point out any symmetrical items, designs, or arrangements that they notice. For example, are the books in the bookcase arranged symmetrically? How about the desks or the windows? Finally, ask students whether or not they see any symmetry anywhere on the United States flag. Students will probably point out the arrangement of the stars in the upper left hand corner of the flag. This part of the flag, tell students, is called the union.

2 Discuss with students the difference between vertical and horizontal lines of symmetry. (You'll find an explanation in "What Students Will Learn" on page 39.) Ask kids which kind(s) of symmetry they see in the union of the flag. (The flag has a vertical line of symmetry. It would also have a horizontal line of symmetry if it weren't for the fact that it is made up of five-pointed stars, all facing the same way!)

3 Distribute a copy of "Stars and Symmetry Forever" on page 43 to each child. Then take a moment to review the flag's history, as presented above. Give children a little time to locate any lines of symmetry that exist in the union of the flags shown, as the worksheet instructions direct.

AND DID YOU KNOW . . .

Over the years, "The Star-Spangled Banner" became more and more popular. In the 1890s, it became the official song of the Army and Navy. 1916, President Woodrow Wilson ordered that it be played on official occasions but not until 1931 did the Congress, by decree, make the song the national anthem of the United States.

4 When they're done, point out to students that, because the two halves of a symmetrical image are the same, they should be able to place a small hand mirror over one half of a symmetrical design and "see" the entire image. (The "mirror image" will take the place of the part that is covered.) If possible, invite students to check their worksheet answers with a small hand mirror this way.

5 Before asking students to follow the directions at the bottom of the worksheet, demonstrate to the children how they can create their own "symmetrical stars" out of construction paper, as described in the box on page 42. If they like, students can then create 13 (or more!) of these to help them experiment with various ways of arranging their stars on a page.

6 When they're done, have students help you create a bulletin board display showing the symmetrical star arrangements that they make.

What Students Will Learn

A line of symmetry is a line where a shape or design can be folded so that its two halves match. If the two halves match when a vertical line is drawn, then the shape is said to have *vertical symmetry*. If the two halves match when a horizontal line is drawn, then the shape is said to be *horizontally symmetrical*. In some cases, the same shape or pattern can be symmetrical both ways, as is the case with the British Union Jack, which was used as the union (the upper, inner corner) of the Grand Union flag, shown below. The Grand Union flag was flown from the winter of 1775 until the first version of the Stars and Stripes was adopted on June 14, 1777. The 13 stripes represented the 13 colonies, while the Union Jack showed that the loyalty of these colonies still resided with the British crown.

Horizontal line of symmetry

Vertical line of symmetry

The Grand
Union flag.

Extensions

Flags, Flags, and More Flags

Invite students to brainstorm other flags that have played an important role in U.S. history. For example, they might mention the role of state flags, the apocryphal story of Betsy Ross and the first flag, the Confederate flags that flew over the Southern states during the Civil War, the flag that was raised on Mount Suribachi at the end of the Battle of Iwo Jima, or the flag that was planted on the moon. Invite students to research, and share with the class, the story behind one or more of these flags, a picture of what they looked like, and a description of which types of symmetry (if any) these flags contain.

You're a Grand Old Shape

Encourage students to see how many regular polygons—such as rectangles, quadrilaterals, or pentagons—they can find on the national flag. Then have them locate a copy of their own state flag for a comparison of the two. (For example, Alabama's state flag is square, Ohio's is in the shape of a swallow-tailed pennant, and Maryland's has lots of differ-ent quadrilaterals on it.) Students can then create their own individual flags, using attributes from both Old Glory and their own state flag. Finally, have each child challenge a classmate to fig-ure out which attributes from each flag the student chose to use in his or her own original flag design.

An Activity with Flying Colors!

Invite students to think of ways that they might be able to estimate what fraction of the United States flag is red, what fraction is white, and what fraction is blue. To fig-ure out what fraction is red, for example, they might start by imagining that the red stripes extended across the entire width of the flag. They can then subtract from their estimate an estimate of the amount of space taken up by half of the union. Have students compare the fractions that they end up with, as well as the methods and thinking they used to arrive at their conclusions. Then, if possible, provide stu-dents with acetate overlays of graph paper to help them modify and fine-tune their estimates. Finally, ask students if they think these fractions would change if the flags they used to make their estimates were larger or smaller. Why or why not? (Since everything on the flag would be enlarged or reduced by the same amount, or in the same proportion, the fraction of each color that appears would also remain the same.)

Try This on for Size

In 1959, when Alaska and Hawaii were added to the Union, the United States flag needed to be redesigned. In Executive Order No. 10834, President Dwight D. Eisenhower included official dimensions for this new flag. According to the provisions of that order, the fly (the length of the flag) is always supposed to be 1.9 times the hoist (the flag's height). The largest official flag is 20 feet wide and 38 feet long, while the smallest is $1\frac{32}{100}$ feet wide and $2\frac{1}{2}$ feet long. Have students test whether these dimensions abide by the President's order. They can also test whether the same is true of your school, classroom, or other available flags. Finally, present students with various hoist lengths, and challenge them to compute the fly lengths (or vice versa), along with the area, and the perimeter of these flags. After making a chart like the one below, students can also look for number patterns—particularly in the hoist, fly, and perimeter columns of the chart.

HOIST	FLY	AREA	PERIMETER
1'	1.9'	1.9'	5.8'
2'	3.8'	7.6'	11.6'
3'	5.7'	17.1'	17.4'
4'	7.6'	30.4'	23.2'
5'	9.5'	47.5'	29.0'
6'	11.4'	68.4'	34.8'
7'	13.3'	93.1'	40.6'
8'	15.2'	121.6'	46.4'
9'	17.1'	153.9'	52.2'
10'	19.0'	190.0'	58.0'
11'	20.9'	229.9'	63.8'

✶ ☆ = ★ + **Worksheet Answers** ✶ ☆ = ★ +

Flag A (Great Star): vertical symmetry; Flag B (Hulbert Flag): vertical and horizontal symmetry; Flag C (North Carolina Militia Flag): horizontal symmetry; Flag D (Star-Spangled Banner): horizontal symmetry (Note, however, that in this flag and in the Fort Sumter flag, perfect horizontal symmetry is ruined by the five-pointed star.); Flag E (Fort Sumter Flag): horizontal and vertical symmetry; Flag F (The Bennington Flag): neither type of symmetry, because of the "76."

Make Some Symmetrical Stars!

To make the second part of the worksheet activity a bit more "hands-on," have students cut out 13 or more "symmetrical stars," using the following instructions. (To make their star arrangements as flag-like as possible, suggest that students use white stars colored or pasted onto a blue background.)

1 Fold a square sheet of paper in half.

2 Holding the paper so that the open side is to your right, make three marks, in the following places:
- one-third down from the top on the right side of the paper (the open edge)
- one-third in from the right side along the bottom of the paper
- one-third up from the bottom on the left side of the paper

3 Connect these points as shown, using a ruler and pencil.

4 Cut along the edges of the half-star that you made. Then unfold your star!

Students can use these stars to experiment with various symmetrical star arrangements. As soon as a student is happy with his or her design, have that student paste or tape the stars in place. Or, if they prefer, students can trace around each star and then reuse the same pieces to look for other symmetrical designs.

The Bookshelf

Nonfiction

- *Stars & Stripes: Our National Flag* by Leonard Everett Fisher (Holiday House, 1993). This very simple picture book contains numerous examples of early American flags, along with a short history of each one.

- *By the Dawn's Early Light: The Story of the Star-Spangled Banner* by Steven Kroll, illustrated by Dan Andreasen (Scholastic, Inc., 1994). This beautiful 40-page picture book tells the story of Francis Scott Key and the United States national anthem.

For Teachers

AND DID YOU KNOW . . .
The U.S. flag is the only national flag in the world that is also the subject of its country's national anthem.

- *So Proudly We Hail: The History of the United States Flag* by Rear Admiral William Rea Furlong and Commodore Byron McCandless (Smithsonian Institution Press, 1981).

- *The History of the United States Flag* by Milo M. Quaife, Melvin J. Weig, and Roy E. Appleman (Harper & Bros., 1961).

Name_____

Stars and Symmetry Forever

Shown below are six flags that have been used, at one time or another, in American history. Take a close look at the union (the box in the upper left hand corner) of each one. Draw in any lines of symmetry that you find.

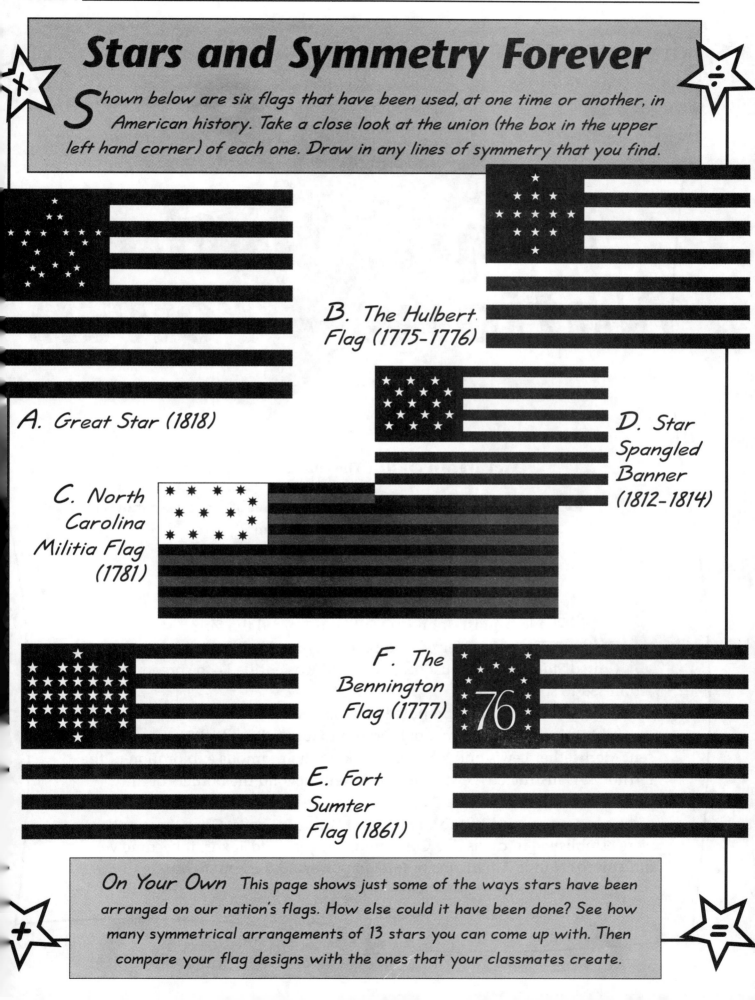

B. The Hulbert Flag (1775-1776)

A. Great Star (1818)

D. Star Spangled Banner (1812-1814)

C. North Carolina Militia Flag (1781)

F. The Bennington Flag (1777)

E. Fort Sumter Flag (1861)

On Your Own This page shows just some of the ways stars have been arranged on our nation's flags. How else could it have been done? See how many symmetrical arrangements of 13 stars you can come up with. Then compare your flag designs with the ones that your classmates create.

ca. 1845
Mapping the Nation's Growth

Key Math Skill   The Four-Color Map Problem

What You'll Need   Blank paper ☆ A set of crayons or markers
for each cooperative group

Historical Background

In 1845, a journalist, John L. O'Sullivan, coined the term "Manifest
Destiny." The term referred to a popularly-held belief of the time that the
United States was not just destined—but was entitled—to spread itself out
"from sea to shining sea."

Perhaps this attitude originated in 1803 with the Louisiana Purchase. Soon
after obtaining this huge tract of land from France, President Thomas Jefferson
sent Meriwether Lewis and William Clark on their famous exploration of the
territory. As instructed, Lewis and Clark went beyond the borders of the
Purchase, all the way to the Pacific. Soon more and more Americans were
setting out on routes like the Oregon and Santa Fe Trails. Once these settlers
were established in areas like California, Oregon, and Texas, it became very
difficult for Native Americans or foreign powers to force them out.

Jefferson

Polk

In 1836, for example, push came to shove in Texas, where American settlers decided that they wanted their independence from Mexico. Although they lost the battle at the Alamo, they soon rallied and became the independent Republic of Texas. Then, in 1845, Congress admitted Texas to the Union as the nation's 28th state.

In 1844, James K. Polk won the presidency on a platform of westward expansion. He negotiated an agreement with the British that divided the Oregon Country at the 49th parallel. Before leaving office in 1849, Polk provoked a war with Mexico that resulted in the United States acquiring all of present-day California, Nevada, and Utah, as well as parts of Arizona, New Mexico, Colorado, and Wyoming. Manifest Destiny was a reality in the United States.

So Where's the Math in That?

Just as a star has to be added to the flag each time a new state joins the Union, a new map is needed each time the territory of a country expands. That has been true many times over in United States history, such as in 1803 when Jefferson acquired the Louisiana Purchase, in 1845 with the annexation of Texas, and again in 1846 when the Oregon Territory was acquired from Britain.

In this activity, students will use historical maps of the United States to analyze a map-making quirk known as the Four-Color Map Problem. They will experiment to determine the fewest number of colors needed so that no two adjoining states are colored the same way.

AND DID YOU KNOW . . .

During the Mexican War, American settlers in California briefly proclaimed their area an independent republic called the Bear Flag Republic. Today the grizzly bear still remains on the California state flag, even though there are no longer any grizzlies in the state.

What to Do

1 After giving children a brief synopsis of Manifest Destiny, as given above, distribute copies of page 48, showing the original 13 colonies. Challenge children to use crayons or markers to figure out the fewest number of colors needed to shade it so that no two adjoining colonies (colonies that touch) are colored in the same way.

2 As a class, discuss the children's experiences trying to solve the problem. Ask: How many students think two colors are needed? Three colors? Four? If discrepancies exist between the children's findings, see if students can resolve them, either in small groups or as a class. (Students should be able to color in this map using a maximum of three colors.)

3 Next, offer students copies of page 49, showing how much the U.S. territories grew between 1783 and 1853. Before coloring in this map, ask students to speculate on the fewest number of colors that they think it will take. (This map should also take three colors to complete.)

HOW THE UNITED STATES GREW: 1783–1853

4 Finally, present students with copies of page 50, showing the 48 contiguous United States as they are today. Again, ask children to take an educated guess about how many colors they think they'll need to complete the map. Before coloring in the map, be sure students understand that, although no two adjoining states can be colored in the same way, states that meet at only one point—such as New Mexico and Utah—can be colored the same. (Students should find that this map will take four different colors to complete.)

5 Next, distribute blank paper and invite students to create their own made-up maps in which only two colors would be needed. (For example, this map might contain only two areas. Or it could be made up of land masses—like stripes on a flag—that are all parallel to each other. Another possibility might be that each area entirely encircles the one next to it, creating a series of rings.)

6 Finally, invite students to see if they can create a map that would require more than four different colors. After giving them a bit of time to experiment, admit to the children that, in 1976, mathematicians were able to prove that it would be impossible to create such a map.

AND DID YOU KNOW . . .

"Four colors suff[...] became the m[...] on the post[...] meter at t[...] University of Illinois, wh[...] Kenneth Appel and Wolf[...] Hanken solved the Fo[...] Color Map Problem in 1976.

What Students Will Learn

As you may know, most mathematical proofs are based on a series of logical steps (i.e., "If A is true, then so is B"). In the Four-Color Map Problem, however, mathematicians were unable to prove their theory relying solely on this process. Instead, they decided that they would have to categorize every conceivable type of map so that they could then test them all, one at a time. By the time this had been accomplished in 1976, the proof had taken some 1,200 hours of computer time. It was also groundbreaking news in the world of mathematics. For the first time in history, a mathematical theorem had been proven with the help of research techniques, rather than just logic.

Obviously it is unrealistic to have students try to recreate this entire process. In this activity, however, they do rely on similar techniques of trial and error. They'll also see how something that might seem fairly obvious can be incredibly difficult to prove.

AND DID YOU KNOW . . .

The California Gold Rush of 1849 gave Americans even more reason to support the concept of Manifest Destiny. That year alone, more than 100,000 adventurers raced west to "get in on the action," which began when James Marshall, a New Jersey mechanic who was building a sawmill for Johann Sutter, spotted yellow flecks of gold shining in the American River, east of San Francisco, California.

Extensions

Check Out These State Shapes

Since they're busy looking at maps of the United States anyway, invite your students to see how many "perfect polygons" they can identify on a map of the United States. For example, how many quadrilaterals—like Colorado and Wyoming—can they identify? Would they consider New Mexico an octagon? Why or why not? What shape name can they use to describe Utah? What about North Dakota? Invite students to see how many other states they can describe solely by their shape.

The Konigsburg Bridge Problem

The Four-Color Map Problem is categorized under a branch of mathematics known as topology, or the study of locations. Another fun topology problem that you may wish to share with students is known as the Konigsburg Bridge problem. This problem originated in an area once known as Konigsburg, but which is now called Kalingrad. It is located on the Preger River, some 60 miles to the east of Gdansk, Poland, in what used to be part of East Prussia. Konigsburg was built on the banks of a river with two islands in the middle. The islands were connected to the mainland, and to each other, by seven bridges, as above.

Townspeople used to wonder if there was a way to cross each bridge only once and still end up where they started. Challenge your students to find a way to do it. They'll find that it is impossible—as a famous mathematician, Leonard Euler, finally proved in 1739.

Konigsburg's seven bridges

The Bookshelf

Nonfiction

• *The Quilt-Block History of Pioneer Days with Projects Kids Can Make* by Mary Cobb (The Millbrook Press, 1995) gives a short description of the settling of America. The bulk of the book, however, focuses on the artistry of quilts.

Fiction

• *Carlota* by Scott O'Dell (Dell Publishing, 1977). In this short novel readers commiserate with Carlota de Zubarán, a 16-year-old Mexican tomboy forced to deal with the invasion by U.S. troops of her California homeland circa 1846.

For Teachers

• "The Solution of the Four-Color Map Problem," by Kenneth Appel and Wolfgang Haken (October 1977 issue, *Scientific American*).

Map A: Color the 13 Colonies

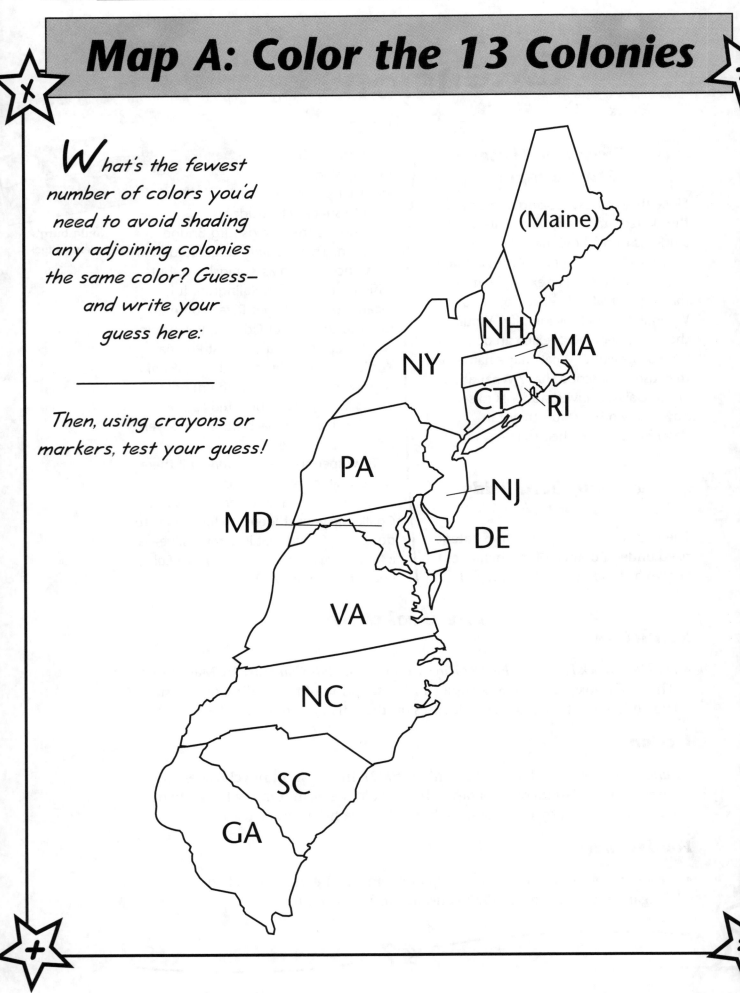

*W*hat's the fewest number of colors you'd need to avoid shading any adjoining colonies the same color? Guess— and write your guess here:

_____

Then, using crayons or markers, test your guess!

(Maine)

NH

NY

MA

CT

RI

PA

NJ

MD

DE

VA

NC

SC

GA

Name_____

Map B: Color the Growing Nation

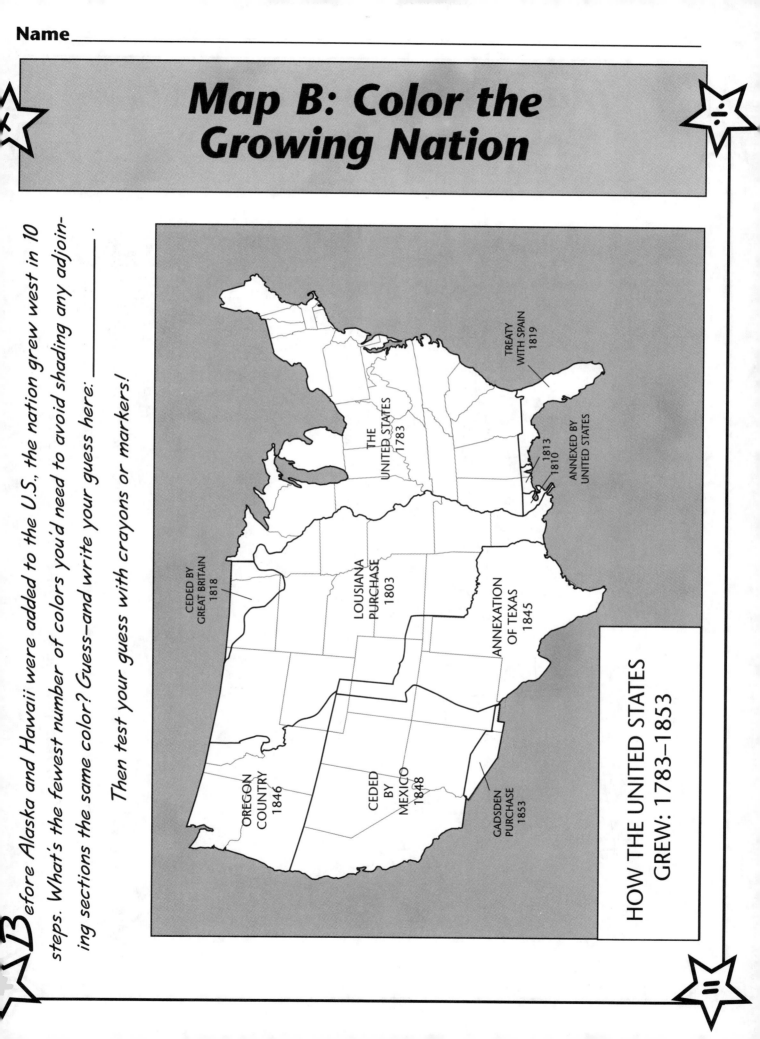

Before Alaska and Hawaii were added to the U.S., the nation grew west in 10 steps. What's the fewest number of colors you'd need to avoid shading any adjoining sections the same color? Guess—and write your guess here: _____ .

Then test your guess with crayons or markers!

TREATY WITH SPAIN 1819

ANNEXED BY UNITED STATES

1813
1810

THE UNITED STATES 1783

CEDED BY GREAT BRITAIN 1818

LOUSIANA PURCHASE 1803

ANNEXATION OF TEXAS 1845

OREGON COUNTRY 1846

CEDED BY MEXICO 1848

GADSDEN PURCHASE 1853

HOW THE UNITED STATES GREW: 1783–1853

Map C: Color the Lower 48 States

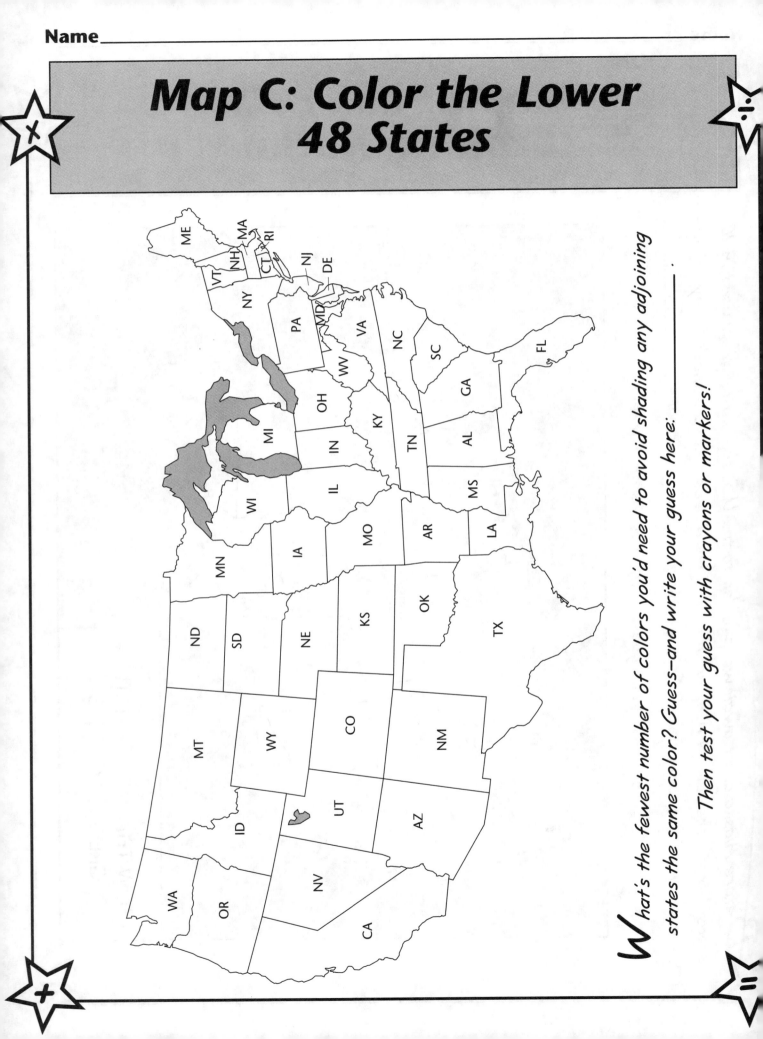

What's the fewest number of colors you'd need to avoid shading any adjoining states the same color? Guess—and write your guess here: _____ .

Then test your guess with crayons or markers!

1852
Math Shortcuts from the One-room Schoolhouse

Key Math Skills   The Rule of Three ☆ Simple proportions ☆ Cross multiplication

What You'll Need   A ruler or tape measure ☆ One or more old math textbooks (if available) ☆ Calculators (optional)

Historical Background

Today, elementary education is taken for granted. It's even required by law for children up to a certain age. But in early colonial days, education was a privilege usually reserved for the wealthy. Most children had to stay home and help their parents with housework and farm chores. Besides, most parents didn't have the money to give their children a good schooling. The idea of a "free" education was virtually unheard of back then.

So how did most children learn to read and write? In the little free time they had, parents would teach children the alphabet. Or occasionally a group of women might run a "dame school," a type of home schooling where small children were taught the catechism along with their ABCs. Eventually, when there were enough people living in an area, residents might chip in to build a school and hire a schoolmaster. In those days, the "three R's" were reading, writing, and religion. Morality, discipline, and good manners were usually stressed over 'rithmetic.

As the colonists began their rebellion against England in the mid-eighteenth century, ideas about education began to change also. These ideas continued to evolve after the American Revolution ended. In 1852, as a sign of the growing importance of education, Massachusetts enacted the first compulsory education law in the country. Before long, similar laws were in effect in nearly every state.

So Where's the Math in That?

As we've seen, mathematics was not always a big part of the American elementary school curriculum. In fact, it wasn't even always taught! Arithmetic (known then as the "art of ciphering") arrived in most classrooms during the 1700s. Eventually, as more and more people became involved in business and industry, the subject's importance grew.

By the end of the nineteenth century, it was not enough to merely know how to add and subtract digits. Money math, mental math, multiplication, division, decimals, fractions, measurement, and other practical applications were being stressed in schools.

One math skill that had a lot of relevance to children's lives back in pioneer days was known as the "Rule of Three." This skill, which has somehow lost its name over the years, involves a cross-product equation in which the goal is to find the fourth term in a simple proportion. In this activity, as students find out what life in a one-room schoolhouse might have been like, they'll also see how the Rule of Three was used.

What to Do

1 Point to a tall tree or pole outside the school building, and ask students to brainstorm ways to estimate its height without climbing it. If there is no tree, pole, or window, challenge children to suggest ways that they could estimate the height of their school building without taking a tape measure and going up on the roof.

2 After students have shared their ideas with classmates, decide as a group which of the students' methods are safe and can realistically be tried. Before getting to these, however, tell students that you are going to show them how people in pioneer days measured the heights of objects that were out of their reach.

3 Explain to students that, in the past, heights were often measured with shadows and a type of math known as proportions. Before cutting down a tree, for example, a pioneer would try to figure out about how far away the highest branches would land when it fell.

$$\frac{\text{stick length}}{\text{stick shadow length}} = \frac{\text{tree height}}{\text{tree shadow length}}$$

To do this, the pioneer would pound a short stick in the ground, or find another short object that he or she could safely measure without climbing. The pioneer would then measure the height of this stick, its shadow, as well as the length of the tree's shadow. Using these measurements, he or she could then set up a simple proportion, like the one above.

4 According to the Rule of Three, proportions like these could be solved using cross-multiplication. The only requirement was that like units, such as all inches or all feet, had to be used. Say, for example, the above-ground part of the stick measured 4 inches, its shadow measured 3 inches, and the tree's shadow measured 12 feet. After 12 feet had been rewritten as 144 inches, these numbers could be plugged into the above equation. The proportion would look like this:

$$\frac{4 \text{ inches}}{3 \text{ inches}} = \frac{x \text{ inches}}{144 \text{ inches}}$$

$$3x = 144 \times 4, \text{ or } 576$$
$$x = 576 \div 3, \text{ or } 192$$

5 Using cross-multiplication, pioneers—or students—could then solve the proportion as illustrated at the right. That means that the tree itself stood about 192 inches—or 16 feet tall.

6 After explaining cross-multiplication and the Rule of Three to students, present them with the opportunity to go outside and use this technique to measure some trees by themselves or with a partner. While they're at it, students can also try out their own methods for measuring heights that are out of reach. (One simple method students might like to try is given in the box on page 54.) Kids can then compare these results with those they arrive at using the Rule of Three.

7 Back in the classroom, have students compare the tree measurements that they came up with. If you'd like, invite students to use their results to make a "Tree-mendous Bar Graph" in which they compare the heights of different types of trees.

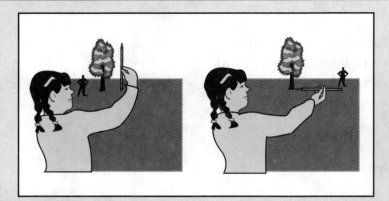

Another Way to Estimate a Tree's Height

- Stand away from the tree, and hold a pencil in front of you, with the point facing up.
- Move the pencil toward you or away from you until it looks like it reaches from the top of the tree to the base. (You may need to close one eye.)
- Keep your arm still, and turn your wrist to the right or left. Stop when the pencil looks level with the ground.
- Have your partner walk from the base of the tree to where your pencil tip appears to reach. He or she should not be walking toward the real pencil, but 90° to the right or left!
- Measure the distance from your partner to the tree. That's about the tree's height.

8 The Rule of Three, tell students, was an important one that students had to learn before graduation. Besides helping them measure trees, it was useful in places like the general store, as the worksheet (page 57) will show them.

9 Distribute the "Ciphering with the Rule of Three" worksheet, and tell students that it contains problems involving the Rule of Three taken from real schoolbooks used in the 1840s. Invite students to try to solve these problems either on their own or with a friend.

What Students Will Learn

By taking part in the hands-on portion of this activity, students will gain a first-hand understanding of simple proportions, cross-multiplication, and the Rule of Three. The worksheet reinforces these skills, and demonstrates additional applications for them.

Extensions

Do a Textbook Comparison

If you have access to both an old and a more recent math textbook, preferably for the same grade, challenge students to do a comparison of the two. Were there any topics that were taught in the past that are not taught today, or vice versa? In what ways was information presented differently? How are the two texts alike? How are formulas like the Rule of Three time-savers like today's calculators? Finally, have students speculate on how a math textbook of the future might look.

A "Mathematics Bee"

After Noah Webster published his first dictionary and a spelling book called *The Grammatical Institute*, spelling bees became popular activities in classrooms during the mid-1800s.

Here are three ideas for "mathematical bees" that you may want to try in class.

1. Have students take turns spelling and defining words such as *fraction, geometry, decimal, symmetry, tangram, whole number, polygon,* and *estimation.* The list can go on and on! Kids remain in the "bee" until they misspell a word or define a word or phrase incorrectly. The last student remaining at the end of the bee wins!

2. Instead of spelling out words, have students take turns solving problems mentally in a "mental math bee." (In the old days, these were often known as "ciphering matches," or "figure downs.") Again, the last child still in the "bee" at the end of the game wins.

3. This last "spelling bee" is a little different from the others in that there is only one right answer. The winner is the child who can most quickly identify the first number that (in sequential order) has the letter *a* in the spelling of its name. (Students may be surprised to discover that the letter *a* does not appear in a number until the words *one thousand*.)

Create a School of the Future

After showing students how a curriculum changes based on the times, challenge students to research the types of careers that experts are now speculating will be most crucial for life in the 21st century. Based on what they find out, invite students to devise a fifth-grade curriculum, describing the subjects—especially the types of math—they think should be taught, and how schools should look, 100 years from now.

Keep a Math Copybook

Before the first math textbooks appeared in the early 1800s, tell students, teachers used to read problems out loud while children wrote them down in their own hand-made "copybooks." Basically, these were old-fashioned assessment portfolios! Children or their schoolmasters made the copybooks by folding sheets of paper into four, stitching them together in the middle (your students can staple them instead), and then cutting the folded edges to form leaves. The last step was to rule the pages of these books with lines. Invite your students to make copybooks of their own and to fill them with the facts and concepts that they learned during this unit, or that they are proudest to have learned this entire year in math class.

The Bookshelf

Nonfiction

- *A Pioneer Sampler: The Daily Life of a Pioneer Family in 1840* by Barbara Greenwood (Ticknor & Fields Books for Young Readers, 1995). Interspersed with accounts of a year in the life of the Robertsons, a fictional pioneer family, are sidebars containing step-by-step instructions about how to dye fabric, "churn" butter, grow a potato plant, and make a fiddle. Math-related activities include how to make a balance scale and a sand clock, and how to measure like a pioneer. More information is also given in this book about the Rule of Three.

Fiction

- *Front Porch Stories at the One-Room School* by Eleanora E. Tate (Bantam Skylark, 1992). This nostalgic novel, set in the present, takes place on the steps of an old one-room school-house, where Matthew J. Cornelius Carson tells stories of growing up in a small town, and attending the local "Colored" school.

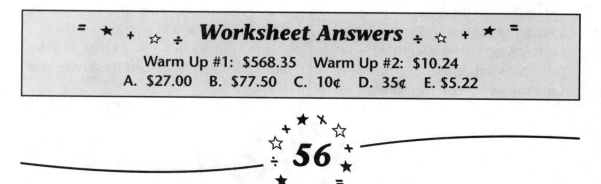

AND DID YOU KNOW . . .
The first schools the United State dedicated t teacher traini were started in the early 1840s. These place were given the name "normal schools."

For Teachers

If you're interested in finding out more about the way the teaching profession evolved within the United States, check out these titles.

- *The Little Red Schoolhouse: A Sketchbook of Early American Education* by Eric Sloane (Doubleday & Co., Inc., 1972). A sweet little book by a man who clearly thought warmly about the simple, unpretentious roots of American education. Included within this nicely illustrated book is a sample page from a math "copybook," similar to those from which the problems on the worksheet were taken.

- *A Forest of Pencils: The Story of Schools through the Ages* by Winifred Trask Lee (The Bobbs-Merrill Co., Inc., 1973). This overview of the history of education goes back even further, covering the ways schools—including math education—have evolved from the days of ancient Rome!

- *Going to School in 1876* by John L. Loeper (Atheneum, 1984). This quick read includes sample diary entries and many other interesting facts about the time period. Some of your students may even enjoy reading this one on their own.

= ★ + ☆ ÷ **Worksheet Answers** ÷ ☆ + ★ =
Warm Up #1: $568.35   Warm Up #2: $10.24
A. $27.00   B. $77.50   C. 10¢   D. 35¢   E. $5.22

Name_____

Ciphering with the Rule of Three

*T**hese** problems were all found hand-written in "copybooks" that date back to the early 1840s.* Aside from the first two warm-ups, the other problems can all be solved using the Rule of Three. To help you get started, the proportion for the first problem is given. See how many of these pioneer problems you can solve!*

WARM UP #1

What will 421 bushels of wheat come to at $1.35 per bushel? _____

WARM UP #2

What will 128 pounds of pork come to at 8¢ per pound? _____

PROBLEMS

A. If 4 bushels of corn be worth $2.25, what is the value of 48 bushels?

$$\frac{4 \text{ bushels}}{48 \text{ bushels}} \qquad \frac{\$2.25}{?}$$

Proportion: _____   Answer: _____

B. What is the value of 124 bushels of apples if 8 bushels be worth $5.00?

Proportion: _____   Answer: _____

C. If 96 pounds of sugar cost $9.60, how much is it per pound?

Proportion: _____   Answer: _____

D. You bought 130 yards of linen for $45.50. What was the price of 1 yard?

Proportion: _____   Answer: _____

E. If 1 yard of muslin cost 12¢, what will $43\frac{1}{2}$ yards cost?

Proportion: _____   Answer: _____

Think About It: Notice that the items and units of weight described in these problems include pounds of pork, bushels of wheat, and yards of muslin. How are these items and measurements similar to, or different from, the items described in your own math textbook? Why do you think that is?

1862
The U.S. Prints Its First Paper Currency

Key Math Skills   Money math ☆ Logic

What You'll Need   Construction paper ☆ Crayons or markers
☆ Calculators (optional)

Historical Background

Money as we know it would be worthless if people refused to view it as "legal tender." During the American Revolution, the colonists began issuing their own money, called "continentals," to help pay the costs of the war effort. So many of these continentals were printed, however, that people began to question their value. Thus, the expression "not worth a continental" was born.

After the war with Great Britain ended, the first United States Bank and the United States Mint were established. A decimal system was agreed upon, and the first official U.S. coins were minted in 1793. In addition, individual state banks often came out with their own paper money. If a bank went out of business, these bills became worthless, generating a distrust of paper money.

During the Civil War the government needed money to pay for supplies and soldiers. For the first time, the government began issuing paper money that could be used anywhere.

The look and size of U.S. currency has changed a lot since the first "greenbacks" were printed in the 1860s. In 1929 their size was reduced 25 percent to their present size. Also, some of the typical American icons once featured on U.S. paper currency—pioneers, Columbus sighting land, and bison—have been replaced with portraits of men like Washington, Lincoln, Franklin, and Grant.

So Where's the Math in That?

In this activity, students will use money math, multiplication with zeros, and logic to match each famous face with the denomination of money on which it appears. In the process, students will learn more facts about American money.

What to Do

1 Discuss with students some of the purposes of money. What did people use before money existed? What other methods could be used to exchange one thing of value for another? Talk about the history of U.S. currency.

2 Have students work in groups to see what kinds of information— especially what types of number facts—are found on dollar bills. Then invite students to help you create a display like the one below.

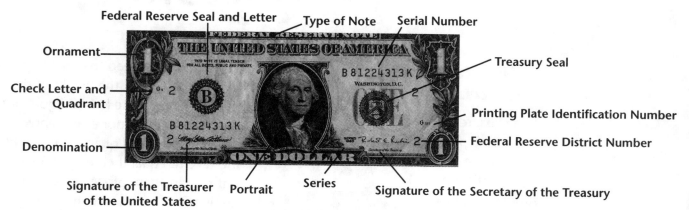

3 Finally, distribute copies of page 62 and allow students to figure out whose face appears on each bill. Go over the worksheet answers as a class. When they're through, divide students into groups and have each research and report on a different person shown on a bill. In their reports, direct students to identify the image on the back of the bill, and explain how it relates to the famous American shown on the other side. (On the back of the $1 bill is the Great Seal of the United States; on the $5 bill is the Lincoln Memorial; the $10 bill shows the U.S. Treasury Building; the $20 bill shows the White House; the $50 bill shows the U.S. Capitol; and on the back of the $100 bill is Independence Hall.)

What Students Will Learn

The worksheet activity provided here gives students plenty of opportunity to use their money multiplication skills. Students will also find that the puzzle goes much faster if they know some "quick tips" about how to multiply with zeros. (For example, multiply the numbers in front of the zeros, then just tack on the total number of zeros at the end. To multiply, say, $500 x $50, multiply the two fives to get $25. Then simply tack on the three remaining zeros for a product of $25,000.)

In addition to exercising their computation skills, students will also need to use some logic to solve this puzzle. For example, once they have plugged in the "givens" of $100, $1,000, and $10,000 onto the appropriate lines, some students may be stuck for a while. If they are, suggest that they figure out which bills cannot be certain amounts. For example, by process of elimination, kids will soon realize that the Madison has to be worth $5,000 because there are no other remaining bills that, multiplied by $2,500 (the number of Madisons that make a Jefferson), will give a money amount that is listed on the chart. From this, kids will then know what amount the Jefferson is worth, and the puzzle should get easier for them from there.

Extensions

How to Really Stretch a Dollar

As a class, read David M. Schwartz's picture book *If You Made a Million*. (See nonfiction book suggestions below.) In that book, Schwartz estimates that a stack of a million one-dollar bills would reach 360 feet into the air. Using this fact, challenge children to estimate about how many $1.00 bills they would need to equal their own height. How about the height of the teacher? Then invite kids to figure out about how much money in pennies, nickels, dimes, and quarters, it would also take to equal their height. Want a hint to start them off? A stack of 50 pennies is about 3 inches high.

How Do You Think Money Should Look?

Over the next few years the face of American money will gradually be changing. The goal is to make it more difficult for counterfeiters to reproduce. After discussing with students what counterfeiting is, and how it can be dangerous to the economy, distribute construction paper and crayons and challenge students to design their own U.S. paper currency. They should consider what, or who, should decorate their own versions of U.S. currency, and what types of elements they might incorporate to help make the money as "counterfeit-proof" as possible. Explain to kids that, before the design of a new bill is approved by the Treasurer of the United States, he or she tries to make sure that it cannot be easily imitated.

Invite each child to take turns presenting his or her own money designs to the rest of the class, who will serve as "the Treasury Department." After everyone has had a chance to present his or her idea for a redesign of the money, have "the Department" vote on which design seems to them to be the most foolproof. They might then do some research to determine what types of anti-counterfeiting steps the United States government really is planning to take.

AND DID YOU KNOW . . . At the end of the Civil War, money printed by the Confederates was suddenly worthless. Today, however, it has value again. That's because numismatists, people who study and collect money from the past, buy them for their historic value.

The Bookshelf

Nonfiction

- *Money, Money, Money: The Meaning of the Art and Symbols on United States Paper Currency* by Nancy Winslow Parker (HarperCollins, 1993).

- *If You Made a Million* by David M. Schwartz (Lothrop, Lee, & Shepard Books, NY, 1989). Helps students appreciate the value of various denominations of money.

For Teachers

- The Federal Reserve Banks offer excellent educational materials on money and banking. For a free *Public Information Materials* catalog, write: Federal Reserve Bank, 33 Liberty Street, Federal Reserve P.O. Station, NY, NY 10045; or call 1-212-270-6130.

- A free booklet on American currency called *Dollar Points* can be obtained by writing: Publications Dept., Federal Reserve Bank at Boston, 600 Atlantic Ave. T-6, Boston, MA 02106.

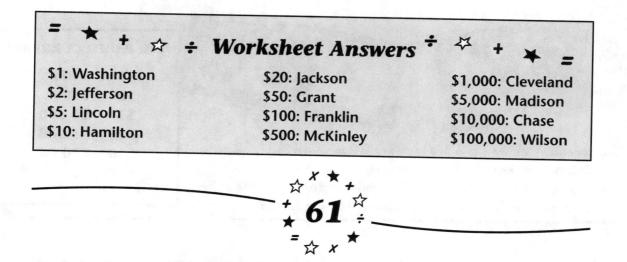

= ★ + ☆ ÷ Worksheet Answers ÷ ☆ + ★ =

$1: Washington	$20: Jackson	$1,000: Cleveland
$2: Jefferson	$50: Grant	$5,000: Madison
$5: Lincoln	$100: Franklin	$10,000: Chase
$10: Hamilton	$500: McKinley	$100,000: Wilson

You Can Bank on It!

Whose face appears on a $1 bill? A $5 bill? A $10 bill? A $20 bill? Use the clues below to match each famous name with one of the 12 types of U.S. paper currency listed in the box below. For example, "$1.00" has already been written next to George Washington's name, because that's the bill on which his face appears.

Clues

✔ It takes 100 Washingtons to make a Franklin, 1,000 Washingtons to make a Cleveland, and 10,000 Washingtons to make a Chase.

✔ It takes 25 Jeffersons to make a Grant, 250 Jeffersons to make a McKinley, and 2,500 Jeffersons to make a Madison.

✔ It takes 2 Hamiltons to make a Jackson and 5,000 Jacksons to make a Wilson.

_$1.00_ **George Washington**	_____ **Benjamin Franklin**
_____ **Abraham Lincoln**	_____ **Alexander Hamilton**
_____ **Thomas Jefferson**	_____ **Andrew Jackson**
_____ **Grover Cleveland**	_____ **Woodrow Wilson**[1]
_____ **Ulysses S. Grant**	_____ **William McKinley**[2]
_____ **Salmon P. Chase**	_____ **James Madison**

1. You'll probably never see a bill showing Woodrow Wilson's picture. Only U.S. government banks still use these bills.
2. Bills showing William McKinley's face have not been printed since 1946. But any that are still around can still be used as cash.

U.S. PAPER CURRENCY

$1	$100
$2	$500
$5	$1,000
$10	$5,000
$20	$10,000
$50	$100,000

ca. 1880
Riding the Santa Fe Railroad West

Key Math Skills   Mental math ☆ Money math

What You'll Need   A local take-out menu for every two kids in the class
☆ Construction paper ☆ Crayons and/or markers

Historical Background

Back in the early days of train travel, there were no dining cars. Travelers either had to bring along their own picnic baskets, or trust their stomachs to the saloons and roadside lunch stands in the towns where the railroads stopped.

Then, along came a man named Fred Harvey. Harvey's dream was to start a chain of railroad-side restaurants with quality food, reasonable prices, and quick service. In 1876 his dream came true when he convinced the owners of the Atchison, Topeka, & Santa Fe Railway that he had a good idea. By the late 1880s, there were more than a dozen Harvey House restaurants along the Santa Fe line from Chicago south to Galveston, Texas, and west to San Francisco, California. Thanks to these eating establishments, the Atchison, Topeka, & Santa Fe sold more tickets west than any of its competitors at that time!

So Where's the Math in That?

Harvey had trouble finding good workers for his restaurants out there in the "wild West." Someone suggested that he bring women from the East to join his staff. The response to his newspaper ads was great! Many women were thrilled to work in a Harvey House restaurant. In general, Harvey found that these women lived up to his high standards, too. "Harvey Girls" always had to be clean, well-mannered, and hard-working. They also had to be able to tally up their customers' bills quickly so that travelers never missed their trains!

In this activity, students will exercise their mental math skills as they role-play the job of waiter or waitress in a Harvey House restaurant. As students' mental math "muscles" improve, they'll be encouraged to increase the difficulty level of the number sets that they try to add in their heads.

What to Do

1 As a warm-up, challenge students to solve a variety of simple math problems without using paper or a pencil:

$25¢ + 15¢ = ?$ $99¢ + 29¢ = ?$ $83¢ + 11¢ = ?$

2 Have students describe some of the strategies that they employ to do this kind of mental math. On the chalkboard, keep a running list of strategies that the children mention. Then add any others that you think it may be helpful for them to know. (See the box on page 65.)

3 Distribute copies of the "Harvey House Lunch Menu" worksheet on page 67, and present students with a brief history of the Harvey House restaurants as described above. Be sure to stress how important fast service—and quick adding abilities—were at these restaurants. If customers missed their trains, they were sure to be mad!

4 Organize students into teams of two students each. Tell the class that in this activity they will take turns playing the role of customer and of server at an old Harvey House restaurant. In the first round of the game, for example, allow the customer to select up to three menu items.

HERE'S ONE WAY TO ESTIMATE A 15% TIP

Say the bill comes to a total of $9.26.

☆ To estimate 10 percent, move the decimal point one place to the left.

Round up or down to the nearest dime.
$9.26 [move decimal] = $0.926
[round to nearest dime] = $0.90

☆ To estimate 5 percent, take $\frac{1}{2}$ of the rounded amount: $0.45

☆ Add the two numbers. That's 15 percent.
$0.45 + $0.90 = $1.35
(If the service is really good, round up to $1.40!)

Mental Math Strategies to Share With Your Students

☆ Count up by 5s, 10s, or by another appropriate number with which you are comfortable. Also, think about the coins and bills which the numbers represent.

Example: 25¢ + 15¢ = 5 nickels + 3 more nickels, or 40¢.

☆ When dealing with numbers or money amounts that end in an 8 or a 9, round up. Then remember to subtract any additional amounts that you added on before announcing your final sum.

Example: 99¢ + 29¢ = $1.00 + 30¢ ($1.30) minus 2¢, or $1.28.

☆ Use place value to help you remember what each digit really means.

Example: 83¢ + 11¢ = 80¢ + 10¢ + 3¢ + 1¢, or 94¢

5 As the server mentally totals the bill, his or her "customer" should keep track of how many minutes or seconds it takes. Later the children can look back at these times to see how their mental math speed has improved.

6 After each round of this game, both players should work together to check the server's answer. Have children keep track of their scores, awarding the server one point for each sum that he or she totals correctly.

7 When all players seem comfortable mentally adding three items, have them work their way up to four, five, and possibly even six items.

8 When you feel your students are ready, distribute a menu from a local restaurant to each team of players. Start by having the "customers" order no more than two items at a time from this menu. (The math here will of course be more difficult since the cost of the items is higher.)

9 Increase the number of items each customer is allowed to choose as your students' mental math skills improve.

What Students Will Learn

Mental math is an important skill that students should be encouraged to master. It's even stressed in the standards that the National Council of Teachers of Mathematics released in 1989. In this activity, students are given the opportunity to practice this skill in levels of increasing difficulty. And they are also given a motivating context in which to do it. Money math skills often come easiest to students because they quickly accept their relevance in their own lives.

Soup............ $1.50
Omelet.......... 3.50
Potatoes........ .75
Ice tea.......... 1.00
             ????

Extensions

It's Hard to Get Good Help These Days

Have students make up an employment "test" for potential Harvey Girl waitresses back in the 1880s. How would students have tested a waitress's mental math? What other abilities might Fred Harvey have required of his hired help? In a few short paragraphs, have students explain what they would have asked a potential waitress during an interview. Make sure children can justify their ideas.

Ready to "Half" Some Lunch?

According to Fred Harvey's original agreement with the Atchison, Topeka & Santa Fe Railway, train crews were entitled to eat at any of his restaurants at half price. Using mental math, ask students to figure out what the most and the least a train operator would have had to pay for a lunch special, a drink and dessert. (The most is 72¢ or 73¢; the least is 25¢.)

Here's a Tip for You . . .

While on the topic of menus and ordering food in a restaurant, explain to students that a tip is a common way to show a waiter or waitress how much you enjoyed your meal. In general, tell students, a 15% tip—or 15¢ on every dollar—is considered proper. Some people, however, leave a little more or a little less, depending on the quality of the service, and of their meal. Use the information on tipping on page 64 to show students how to estimate a 15% tip. Then invite them to figure out what they would have left their waiter or waitress for some of their own made-up menu orders.

The Bookshelf

Nonfiction

• *The Harvey Girls: The Women Who Civilized the West* by Juddi Morris (Walker and Company, 1994). Fred Harvey and the waitresses who worked for him.

Fiction

• *Bonanza Girl* by Patricia Beatty (William Morrow Junior Books, 1962; updated in 1993). After her father dies, 13-year-old Ann Katie Scott, her mother and her brother pack up and move to Idaho Territory, where they open a restaurant.

For Teachers

• *The Harvey Girls: Women Who Opened the West* by Lesley Poling-Kempes (Paragon House, 1989). The appendix contains samples of menus.

Name_____

Harvey House Lunch Menu

Relishes (Appetizers)

Fruit Supreme	. . . . .35¢	Celery Hearts	. . . . 30¢
Radishes	. . . . .15¢	Mixed Olives	. . . . 20¢
Fresh Shrimp Cocktail	. . . . .50¢		

Sandwiches

Cream Cheese and Apple Sauce . . . . 20¢
Hot Young Native Turkey Sandwich . . . . 60¢

Today's Specials

Chili con Carne . . . . 25¢
Frankfurters and Hot Potato Salad . . . . 45¢
Club Steak Smothered with Onions . . . . 90¢
Roast Prime Ribs of Beef au Jus . . . . 75¢

Beverages

Coffee per cup	. . . . 10¢	Tea per pot	. . . . 15¢
Coffee per pot	. . . . 20¢	Malted Milk	. . . . 25¢
Milk per bottle	. . . . 10¢		

Desserts

Ice Cream (Pineapple or Vanilla) . . . . 20¢

Frozen Eclair . . . . 30¢   Raisin Pie . . . . 15¢

Adapted from the menu used at the Harvey House restaurant in Alvarado, New Mexico, January 4, 1929.

1886 The Statue of Liberty

Key Math Skills   Standard units of measurement ☆ Logic ☆ Scale ☆ Ratio and proportion

What You'll Need   String ☆ A ruler or tape measure

Historical Background

Back in 1776, Ben Franklin was sent to France on a mission. His job: To convince the French government to support the 13 colonies in their fight for independence from British rule. With some cajoling, the French agreed to help the budding nation. Without this assistance, many believe the American colonists would have surely failed to gain independence.

Inspired by the American Revolution, the French people soon launched a war against their own monarchy. This French Revolution was to last longer than the American Revolution did. Even by the mid-1800s, France was still undergoing a lot of changes, seeking to find and keep in place a fair and stable government. In the hope that his country might again draw inspiration from America, a scholar, Edouard de Laboulaye, proposed presenting as a gift to the United States a sculpture dedicated to the ideal of Liberty. Frederic-Auguste Bartholdi, a well-known French sculptor, decided to create the statue himself.

So Where's the Math in That?

It would be many years before Laboulaye's and Bartholdi's dreams would become a reality. Many things had to happen first. For one thing, Bartholdi had to make sure that the United States would accept the gift and donate land for the statue to stand on. He and his friends would also have to raise a lot of money to pay for the cost of labor and supplies.

Of course, the other thing Bartholdi still had to do was actually build the statue. This alone would take years of effort—and lots of math! Once Bartholdi had decided what the statue would look like, he built his first model of it. This model stood just a little over 4 feet tall; probably about the same height as some of your students. Bartholdi then made some more models, each one increasingly larger than the one before it. The real statue, when it was completed, would wind up standing more than 27 times the original model's height!

In this activity students will use logic and standard measurement to find out some of Miss Liberty's dimensions. They will also get an idea of how artists use math to make the proportions of their pictures and statues appear lifelike.

What to Do

1 Explain to students that Bartholdi needed lots of measurements to make sure that, despite her size, Miss Liberty would look like a real person. To do this, he took great care to make sure that all her parts would be proportionate to all other parts, and that they would be proportionate to the dimensions of a real human, too.

2 To demonstrate what proportion is, have each child cut a piece of string the length of a partner's head, from the top of the forehead to the tip of the chin. Then invite students to measure the partner's height, arm length, and/or shoulder width using that person's own "head strings."

3 In a class discussion, have kids compare the "head string" measurements that they came up with. Chances are, most kids in your class turned out to be approximately the same number of "heads" tall. Remind students that, even though everyone in the class is a different height—and has a different head size—their proportions are very similar. For example, everyone is probably about seven or eight of his or her own head lengths tall.

4 Once students have the basic idea about what proportion is, distribute copies of the "Miss Liberty—From Toes to Torch" worksheet on page 72, and have children work on it individually or with a partner. If necessary, review equivalent units of measurement—particularly inches and feet.

What Students Will Learn

Without realizing it, students who complete the worksheet activity will have engaged in a simple algebra problem. To do it, they should start with the measurement that they already know—namely, the width of Miss Liberty's head, from ear to ear. By plugging that fact into other clues in the puzzle, children can gradually find out the length of other body parts until eventually the whole problem is solved.

As they work, students will gain a good deal of practice renaming inches as feet and inches, and vice versa. For example, since 12 inches is equal to 1 foot, then 13 inches is equal to 1 foot, 1 inch; 14 inches is equal to 1 foot, 2 inches; and 24 inches is equal to exactly 2 feet. By using a piece of string to compare parts of their own body, students will also gain a basic understanding of ratio and proportion.

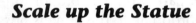

Extensions

Scale up the Statue

To complete this activity, each student will need two sheets of graph paper. The grids on one sheet should be slightly larger than on the other. Using the sheet with the smaller squares, have students draw a simple picture; perhaps even a simplified drawing of the Statue of Liberty. Then challenge kids to redraw the picture on the other piece of graph paper, copying the illustration one square at a time. When they're done, students should have slightly enlarged copies of their own pictures. Explain to students that Bartholdi used a similar method to make larger and larger versions of his statue model. The main difference is that Bartholdi was doing this with a three-dimensional grid!

Match Your Proportions with Miss Liberty's

Point out to students that a few of the measurement clues given on the worksheet are related to proportion. By using these facts, kids can compare their own proportions with those of the statue. For example, according to the worksheet, it would take four of Miss Liberty's eye lengths to equal the distance from one of her ears to the other. Students can then estimate about out how many of their own eye widths it would take to equal the distance between their ears.

You've Got a Great Head on Your Shoulders!

The sculptures on Mount Rushmore in South Dakota are not nearly as tall as the Statue of Liberty. But then again, this granite tribute to Presidents Washington, Lincoln, Jefferson, and Theodore Roosevelt only shows the front of these men's heads. From the chin to the crown, each face carved on Mount Rushmore is about 60 feet high. That's more than three times the height of Lady Liberty's head! If you like, challenge your students to use their knowledge of Lady Liberty's proportions to figure out about how tall each figure on Mount Rushmore would be if their whole bodies were added to the mountain, carved out in proportion to their heads.

The Bookshelf

Nonfiction

- *How They Built the Statue of Liberty* by Mary J. Shapiro (Random House, 1985). This book contains technical information (including how scale was used to build the final statue), presented in a way that most kids will understand.

Fiction

- *Lily and Miss Liberty* by Carla Stevens (Scholastic Inc., 1992). This book, set in New York in 1885, tells the story of a young immigrant girl who finds an original way to raise money to help pay for the Statue of Liberty's pedestal.

For Teachers

- *Math Bridges to Literature: The Story of the Statue of Liberty* (The Continental Press, Inc., 1994). This short eight-page teaching guide suggests math activities for children to do after reading *The Story of the Statue of Liberty* by Betsy and Giulio Maestro (A Mulberry Paperback Book, 1986).

★ + ☆ ÷ ★ **Worksheet Answers** ★ ÷ ☆ + ★

Head from chin to top: 17 feet, 3 inches; head from ear to ear: 10 feet; length of right arm: 42 feet; longest ray in crown: 11 feet, 6 inches; width of mouth: 3 feet; length of torch: 21 feet; width of one eye: 2 feet, 6 inches; length of nose: 4 feet, 6 inches.

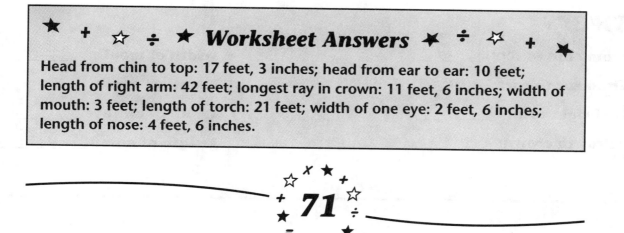

Miss Liberty— From Toes to Torch

*A*re you as tall as the Statue of Liberty's nose is long? Use the clues below to figure it out! While you're at it, you'll find out some other fun measurement facts about the Statue of Liberty. Here's how:

✔ **First, read all of the clues. Somewhere within these clues, one of Lady Liberty's measurements is already given.**

✔ **Write this measurement in the correct space at the bottom of the page.**

✔ **Use the fact you found, along with another clue, to figure out what another part of the Statue of Liberty measures.**

✔ **Keep doing this until you've filled in all of the blanks below.**

Clues

○ **You could line up four of Lady Liberty's eyes to equal the distance from one of her ears to the other.**

○ **The distance from the top of Miss Liberty's head to her chin is 7 feet, 3 inches longer than the distance across her head from ear to ear.**

○ **The torch is half the length of the statue's right arm.**

○ **It would take $1\frac{1}{2}$ times the width of her mouth to equal the length of her nose.**

○ **The width of her mouth is $\frac{1}{7}$ the length of her torch.**

○ **Her nose is exactly 2 feet longer than the distance across either of her eyes, and 7 feet shorter than the longest ray in her crown.**

○ **From ear to ear, Miss Liberty measures 120 inches. (Hint: To get started, figure out how many feet that is.)**

Answers

Head from chin to top: _____

Head from ear to ear: _____

Length of right arm: _____

Longest ray in crown: _____

Width of mouth: _____

Length of torch: _____

Width of one eye: _____

Length of nose: _____

Pictures by David Hockney

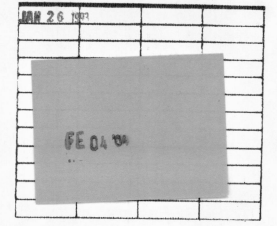

Pictures by David Hockney

Selected and edited by
Nikos Stangos

Harry N. Abrams, Inc., Publishers, New York

Title page photograph by David Hockney taken in his
London studio (1977) with Gregory Evans, his model, on
the couch (left), in front of *Self Portrait with Blue Guitar*,
and, on the right, *Model with Unfinished Self Portrait*
(unfinished state).

International Standard Book Number: 0–8109–2223–1
Library of Congress Catalog Card Number: 79–51615

© 1976 and 1979 David Hockney

Published in 1979 by Harry N. Abrams, Incorporated,
New York
All rights reserved. No part of the contents of this book
may be reproduced without the written permission of
the publishers

Printed and bound in Great Britain by Balding & Mansell,
Wisbech, Cambs.
Filmset in Great Britain by Keyspools Limited, Golborne,
Lancashire

Contents

Introduction by David Hockney

It is very good advice to believe only what an artist does, rather than what he says about his work. Any respectable art historian would never go only by an artist's words; he would look for evidence of them in his work. I think it was Sickert who said somewhere, Never believe what an artist says, only what he does; then he proceeded to write a book. After an artist has done the work, it's reasonably easy to theorize about it, but to theorize about it beforehand could be disastrous. I don't think one should do it even if one has the inclination. People interested in painting might be fascinated by an artist's statements about his work, but I don't think one can rely on that alone to learn about an artist's work, which is all trial and error.

I was born in Bradford in 1937. Until I was eleven, I went to the local council school, where my brothers and sister went. Then I went to Bradford Grammar School on a scholarship. I wasn't really happy there; I was probably too bored. At the age of eleven I'd decided, in my mind, that I wanted to be an artist, but the meaning of the word 'artist' to me then was very vague – the man who made Christmas cards was an artist, the man who painted posters was an artist, the man who just did lettering for posters was an artist. Anyone was an artist who in his job had to pick up a brush and paint something.

It's difficult to say *why* I decided I wanted to be an artist. Obviously, I had some facility, more than other people, but sometimes facility comes because one is more interested in looking at things, examining them, and making a representation of them, more interested in the visual world, than other people are. When I was eleven, the only art you saw in a town like Bradford was the art of painting posters and signs. This was how one made one's living as an artist, I thought. The idea of an artist just spending his time painting pictures, for himself, didn't really occur to me. Of course I knew there were paintings you saw in books and in galleries, but I thought they were done in the evenings, when the artists had finished painting the signs or the Christmas cards or whatever they made their living from.

My father had a slight interest in art. He didn't know much about pictures, but he had attended evening classes at the art school in Bradford in the twenties and thirties, which meant he'd been interested enough to try his hand at drawing and painting. When I was eleven, my father was painting old bicycles; just after the war you couldn't buy new bicycles – they were all exported – so my father used to buy old ones and paint them up to look like new. I used to watch him do it. The fascination of the brush dipping in the paint, putting it on, I love that, even now, I loved it then. There's something about it – I think anyone who makes pictures loves it, it is a marvellous thing to dip a brush into paint and make marks on anything, even on a bicycle, the feel of a thick brush full of paint coating something. Even now, I could spend the whole day painting a door just one flat colour.

My father obviously enjoyed doing that kind of thing. I remember in about 1950 he decided to modernize the house. He began by putting a whole sheet of hardboard flush over each of the panelled doors, and then he painted sunsets on the doors – sunsets that looked as if they were wood-veneer pictures. He painted all the doors like this, and I thought they were wonderful. He also used to paint posters a little bit. He was quite good at lettering. In those days, there were people who could do very quick hand-lettering; there was a demand

Self-Portrait with Blue Guitar, 1977. Oil on canvas, 60 × 72 (153 × 183).

for it. Posters advertising films were painted by hand. I would go up and look to see how they were done. You could still see the brush marks. People also did little signs for restaurants and cafés. To me this was the work of a real artist.

At Bradford Grammar School we had just an hour and a half of art classes a week in the first year; after that you went in for either classics or science or modern languages and you did *not* study art. I thought that was terrible. You could only study it if you were in the bottom form and did a general course. So I said Well, I'll be in the general form, if you don't mind. It was quite easy to arrange, because if you did less work you were automatically put in that section. I remember the mathematics teacher used to have some little cacti on the window sill; I always thought I never needed to listen in those classes, and I used to just sit at the back and secretly draw the cacti. Then they told me off for not doing much work, and the headmaster said Why are you so lazy? You got a scholarship. When I pointed out that I wanted to do art, they told me There's plenty of time for that *later*.

I think it's a very bad thing people aren't made to study art. Whole generations of people in England went to schools where they had no visual education, and you can see the results all around us. Visual education is treated as if it's quite unimportant, but it's of vast importance because the things we see around us affect us all our lives. After the first year at the Grammar School you didn't do any more art until you got into the sixth form, when you did art appreciation, and I think that's a little bit late. Even if one isn't going to be an artist – of course, most people aren't going to be artists – art training sharpens the visual sense, and if people's visual sense is sharp you get beautiful things around you, whereas if it's not they don't care about their surroundings. It makes a vast difference to a city, to a country.

The art master used to be encouraging, and so did a man who taught English. Once we were supposed to write an essay on some subject, and I hadn't done it because I'd spent all my time making a collage self portrait for the art class. So when he said Where is your essay? Can I read it out? I had the collage with me for the art class and – I was, I suppose, a cheeky schoolboy – I said I haven't done the essay, but I've done this. And he looked at the collage, and he said Oh, it's marvellous. I was so taken aback because I expected him to say You terrible person.

At the school there was an art society which met in the evenings, and I used to go to that. The school magazine always had a report about the various societies, and I remember in my very first term the report on the art society said 'Hockney D. provided light relief.' I was about eleven, and I didn't know what 'light relief' was; it sounded like sculpture to me – I thought maybe that was what I'd been doing there.

I wanted to go to the junior art school, attached to Bradford School of Art, when I was fourteen, but the scholarship people wouldn't let me leave the Grammar School and the headmaster said It's silly, and you need this education. I hated them for making me stay. I left immediately I was sixteen. My parents were a bit reluctant to let me start at art school then, because when my brothers left school they had gone out to work. Their worries were only financial, that's all. I said Oh, it's essential to go to art school; to be an artist you have to be trained. But my mother said Well, why don't you go and try to get a job in a commercial art studio in Leeds? She sent some little drawings up to London, to the National Council for Design, or something, and she got a letter back saying No, they were no good at all. And so I said – I was quite pleased – It means, you see, you have to go to art school to learn. But I did try to get a job. I made up a little portfolio; I did some lettering and other things I thought commercial artists would do. I took it round some studios in Leeds and finally one of them said Well, we could give you a job, but you would be better off going to art school. And I said Oh, I know. Then they told me they might give me a job, but I said No, maybe I'll go to art school, I'll take your advice. I went back home and told my mother they said I must go to art school even if it's just for a year. She seemed convinced, so I started at the School of Art in Bradford.

When I started at the art school, they said Well, you should do commercial art. At first I was ready to do anything they suggested, I was so pleased to get in there, but after I'd been there three or four weeks I realized that really I'd be better off saying I wanted to do painting because all you did then was drawing and painting, especially from life. Most of the students on this course said they wanted to be teachers – it was regarded as the teacher training course. I told them I wanted to change to the painting course. Ah, you want to be a teacher. No, no, I said, an artist – it seemed to me to be giving in already if you said 'teacher'. I thought you should teach only after you had practised the art for a while on your own; otherwise you wouldn't know what to teach. They tried again to put me off; they said Do you have a private income? I said What's that? I don't know what a private income is. They said You'll never make a living as a painter. Most people never will but, again, it seems a rotten thing to say to somebody of sixteen, if he's keen. *I* would never say that to somebody of sixteen. Anyway, I wasn't put off, and I changed to the course for the National Diploma in Design. You studied a main subject and a subsidiary subject for two years; my main subject was painting, and my subsidiary was lithography. Then the last two years you could specialize in one subject which for me was painting. It meant that for four years all you did was draw and paint, mostly from life; for two days a week you did life painting, two days a week what they called figure composition, which had to be realistic, from life, and one day a week drawing. During the first two years one day a week was devoted either to perspective or anatomy. The training was completely academic. In the last year a lady gave a few lectures on art history and for your final examination you had to write an essay on an artist or a school of painting.

I was interested in everything at first. I was an innocent little boy of sixteen and I believed everything they told me, everything. If they said You have to study perspective, I'd study perspective; if they told me to study anatomy, I'd study anatomy. It was thrilling, after being at the Grammar School, to be at a school where I knew I would enjoy everything they asked me to do. I loved it all and I used to spend twelve hours a day in the art school. For four years I spent twelve hours there every day. There were classes from nine-thirty to twelve-thirty, from two to four-thirty and from five to seven; then there were night-classes from seven to nine, for older people coming in from the outside. If you were a full-time student you could stay for those as well; they always had a model, so I just stayed and drew all the time right through to nine o'clock.

What you look at is important when you are that young. Most of the art I saw was at the art school. In those days there were very few art books and the library was very small; I can remember the arrival of the first big art books with colour pictures, the Skira books from Switzerland. I pored over them – they were books on nineteenth-century French painting, the impressionists. I didn't make my first trip to London until I was nineteen, which meant the only *real* paintings I'd ever seen were in Bradford, Leeds, Manchester and York. The Leeds Art Gallery had quite good pictures. In those days they had the great big Rembrandt equestrian picture which is now in the National Gallery, and they had one or two French pictures, and Flemish ones. The only contemporary art we saw was English. In my last year, when we'd already done a lot of drawing, I realized how academic the art school was and I began to think, the whole problem is, I don't know anything about modern art. They liked Sickert; Sickert was the great god and the whole style of painting in that art school – and in every other art school in England – was a cross between Sickert and the Euston Road School. By the time I was leaving, I'd started having doubts as to what was valuable: had I really done anything valuable? Had the time been wasted? Well, of course, it's really a bit silly asking a twenty-year-old whether he has wasted his time or not. Anyway, these doubts were raised in me because I'd become more aware of contemporary art.

Portrait of My Father is almost the first oil painting I ever did. It was painted at home on Saturday afternoons when my father had finished work. In the last two summers I was at

Bradford I used to paint out of doors. I did a number of little pictures of semi-detached houses, Bradford suburbs. I put all the paints on a little cart made from a pram, wheeled it out and painted on the spot. And they loved my pictures at the art school; they thought they were quite clever. But *Portrait of My Father* was *sold*. I sent that and another picture of the street where I lived in Bradford to an exhibition in Leeds, in 1954 I think, the Yorkshire Artists Exhibition, which was held every two years in the Leeds Art Gallery for local Yorkshire artists. It was a big event. All the staff of the art school sent pictures and most of the paintings were made up of the graduate fellows there, who were regarded as highly professional. Most of the other pictures were by teachers of local art schools. When I sent these two pictures, I didn't even bother putting a price on them; I thought, no one will buy them anyway.

I remember going to the opening on a Saturday afternoon. They had free sandwiches and tea and I thought it was a great event, an enormous event. A man at the opening saw *Portrait of My Father*, found out that a young boy had done it, and offered me ten pounds for it; I was amazed! It was a great deal of money and as my father had bought the canvas I thought, it's really *his* painting, it's his canvas – I'd just done the marks on it. So I phoned him up and said There's a man who'd like to buy this picture, can I sell it? And he said Ooh, yes. He thought it was because it was of *him*, you see, and he said You can do another. So I said Yes, all right. I had to buy drinks for everybody at the art school the next Monday. That probably cost a pound. The idea of spending a whole pound in a pub seemed absurd, but with the rest of the ten pounds I got some more canvas and painted some more pictures and then I exhibited them, in local exhibitions in Bradford and Leeds, mostly. The paintings are mostly oils. Doing an oil painting was considered advanced, and a painting three feet by four feet was considered then to be a major canvas you were going to be slaving away at for a long time.

When I painted *Portrait of My Father*, my father, who'd bought the canvas, set up the easel and then set the chair up for himself, and he set mirrors round so he could watch the progress of the painting and give a commentary. And he would say Ooh, that's too muddy, is that for my cheek? No, no, it's not that colour. I had this commentary all the time, and I'd say Oh, no, you're wrong, this is how you have to do it, this is how they paint at the art school, and I carried on. You aimed at likeness, but what you were really concerned about were tonal values – tone – making sure you'd got the right tone. This meant you ignored colour. Colour was not a subject of painting in the art school.

After leaving the art school in 1957 I had to do national service, and I objected to doing it. I thought of myself as a pacifist then, and I went and worked for one year at the hospital in Bradford. Then I moved. I rented a cottage at St Leonard's-on-Sea in Sussex, and worked at a hospital in Hastings. For two years I did very little work.

I read Proust for eighteen months, which is probably another reason I didn't do any work. I *made* myself read it because at first it was much too difficult. I'd never been abroad, but I'd been told it was one of the great works of art of the twentieth century. I'd read from an early age, but mostly English. So long as it was about England, I had some sense of what it was about. Dickens I'd read and you had some sense of what it was, but Proust was different. I remember asparagus was mentioned in it; I had no idea what asparagus was. I've since read it again, and I realize I couldn't have got much from reading it the first time.

In 1957 I had applied to the Royal College of Art and the Slade with life drawings, life paintings and figure compositions, paintings I'd done at the art school and at home during holidays. Anybody who'd studied painting in art school in those days would then apply either to the Royal College or the Slade or the Royal Academy, which were post-graduate schools; what one learned at art school wasn't sufficient. I was really glad to get back to art school and I was determined to work hard again. I'd been accepted in the Royal College painting department. Ron Kitaj was in the same year, and Allen Jones, Derek Boshier, Peter Phillips.

Soon after I started at the Royal College, the kind of paintings I did changed: in those two years of doing hospital work, although I hadn't done any painting, naturally I'd been thinking about it. In my last year at Bradford School of Art I made three or four trips to London and looked at things in the Tate Gallery, the National Gallery. I was young, and all young people are more interested in the art of their immediate time – old Michelangelo, you know, you don't quite see it and understand it.

It was only then, in a way, I'd begun to discover Picasso. In the fifties in England, there was still, especially if you lived in the provinces, a mile of philistinism about Picasso. It's disappeared now. For instance, Alfred Munnings, the horse painter, was always referring to Picasso as an awful, terrible artist, and things like that. I remember reading once that Picasso had said Who is this Sir Munnings? At the time I realized people were just being philistine and the art was obviously much better than anything they were doing. Yet it was quite difficult sorting it out, and so when I started at the Royal College of Art I honestly did not know what to do. I realized it was no good going on painting as I had been; I felt I wanted to do something else. I didn't even have any strong preferences about the modern art I had seen. I was very open. I'd become quite a lover of Picasso though. It'd begun to have quite an effect. I think the very first Picassos I'd liked were from the late thirties: *Weeping Woman*, I remember, was a picture I began to really admire. It was these thirties Picasso paintings and *Guernica* that, I began to realize, I had to take notice of myself. They were great significant pictures and if you were studying painting you had to take notice of them.

Immediately after I started at the Royal College, I realized that there were two groups of students there: a traditional group who simply carried on as they had done in art school, doing still life, life painting and figure compositions; and then what I thought of as the more adventurous lively students, the brightest ones, who were more involved in the art of their time. They were doing big abstract expressionist paintings on hardboard.

The first student I got to know there was Ron Kitaj. We got on immediately. Also, his painting straightaway fascinated me. I could tell he knew more about painting than anybody else. He's about four years older than I am, which when you're twenty-two is a lot of difference, in experience anyway. He was a much more serious student than anybody else there. He has a marvellous dry humour that really appeals, but in those days he was much grimmer than he is now, and he was a rather formidable person. He used to put up a kind of front against people as though he couldn't tolerate fools. I got on with him because we had a few things in common. Literature we would talk about; he was interested in Orwell, and I remember talking to him about *The Road to Wigan Pier* which I knew very well as a book from a long time ago. It was written in the year I was born, and my father was always mentioning it; he'd say It was written in the year you were born, and this is what it was like. Ron was a great influence on me, far more than any other factor; not just stylistically – he was a great influence stylistically on a lot of people, and certainly on me – but in his seriousness too. Painting was something that you were studying seriously. A lot of people thought art students were serious in that way, but they weren't; they just gassed around, and I always thought that was silly. The painters teaching at the College left you fairly free, as long as you did drawing, because in those days that was still compulsory – which was fine with me. I'd always liked drawing a figure. Some people hate it, they don't want to do it; I'd always liked it, partly because I've always been able to do it; but I worked at it. Everybody else was doing big abstract expressionist pictures. And I thought, well, that's what you've got to do.

In 1956 there'd been a big exhibition at the Tate of American abstract expressionist painting, and then Bryan Robertson had done shows at the Whitechapel of Pollock and in 1961 Rothko. And this was the latest thing. This was painting that had been done just two or three years before in America. Young students had realized that American painting was more interesting than French painting. The idea of French painting disappeared really, and

American abstract expressionism was the great influence. So I tried my hand at it, I did a few pictures, about twenty on three feet by four feet pieces of hardboard that were based on a kind of mixture of Alan Davie cum Jackson Pollock cum Roger Hilton. And I did them for a while, and then I couldn't. It was too barren for me.

Meanwhile, I was drawing all the time. The one student I kept talking to a lot was Ron Kitaj. Ron was slowly doing these strange pictures, and I talked to him about them and about my work. And I said Well, I don't know, it seems pointless doing it. I'd talk to him about my interests; I was a keen vegetarian then, and interested in politics a bit, and he'd say to me Why don't you paint those subjects? And I thought, it's quite right; that's what I'm complaining about, I'm not doing anything that's from me. So that was the way I broke it. I began to paint those subjects. But I still hadn't the nerve to paint figure pictures; the idea of figure pictures was considered really anti-modern, so my solution was to begin using words. I started writing on the pictures. And when you put a word on a painting, it has a similar effect in a way to a figure; it's a little bit of human thing that you immediately read; it's not just paint. The idea came because I didn't have the courage to paint a real figure, so I thought, I have to make it clear, so I'll write 'Gandhi' on this picture about Gandhi. I can remember people coming round and saying That's ridiculous, writing on pictures, you know, it's mad what you're doing. And I thought, well, it's better; I feel better; you feel as if something's coming out. And then Ron said Yes, that's much more interesting.

I wrote a little piece the other day for a catalogue of a show in Los Angeles, just a very short thing about painting (I'm rather against painters making big polemical statements in catalogues. I've never done it myself. There are a few vague ones, that's all. From experience I know they become things that are very heavily quoted). I said I felt I was quite a traditional artist and painter in the sense that to me paintings should have content. I said my paintings have content, always a subject and a little bit of form. And I was traditional in the sense that I felt you should have a balance between these two to make a really good painting. If you didn't (I didn't add it but inferred it), the painting would become boring, in the sense that English Victorian painting is – it can be very charming and it wasn't as bad as people think, but the weakness of it is that its real emphasis is on content as opposed to form. The weakness of a lot of paintings today, of the last ten years, is just the reverse: that their emphasis has been totally on form and not on content. It seems to me that really great pictures – and I'm interested in making *pictures* – must achieve a balance. Take Rembrandt, or anybody we admire: his achievement is the balance between content and form; it's not just form.

What I'm talking about of course is a permanent problem in painting, which probably will never be solved in theory. For instance, look at Piero della Francesca's wonderful pictures that are marvellous and exciting to look at, that delight you. I would think anybody who likes painting at all would like a Piero della Francesca; I couldn't imagine anybody thinking they were awful in any way. Each picture, as far as I know, has a very definite subject; I think every one is a Christian story, isn't it? Yet our delight in the pictures is in the way they're constructed; that's what makes them stand out, not the story. But the problem is that we don't know, we can never tell, how much the subject, in an old fashioned way, inspired these things. It's common knowledge that artists, certain artists, need a subject, that a subject can be inspiring. It's true in literature and it's true in painting. Some artists need subjects more than others, but you can play down the subject too much; there is an importance in it. In the 1960s the subject had been completely played down; abstraction had begun to dominate everything, and people firmly believed that this was the way painting had to go. There was no other way out, people thought. Even I felt that, and I still felt it even when I began to reject it in action; in theory I still couldn't reject it at all. I felt, well, I'm sure they're right, and I think I felt that even as late as 1966. It was in 1965 I painted probably some of the most abstract pictures I'd done, influenced, I think, by American abstraction, what they called American cool abstraction. But of course what made it very different was that I was using abstraction as my subject, commenting on it – I felt the *need* to use it as a subject. I must admit I think the reason my paintings did have quite an appeal was that, first of all, people could write something about them. If you're writing about a Franz Kline painting, for instance, on the whole you're writing about formal values and gestures. You can always talk about formal values in a figurative picture, but there are other things. And that makes it easier for people to write about pictures. On the other hand, you have painters like Barnett Newman; if you compare Newman as a painter to, say, Degas, I think you can see that Newman is concerned more with ideas – obsessively so, because he's not as good an artist as Degas. He is more concerned with theory as well, though Degas was too – any good artist is, actually; you can't ignore it. But it's Degas's eye and attitudes that matter, the responses he got, the responses he in part *felt*. In Barnett Newman's work it isn't like that at all. I'm not praising one over another, we all know who is the better artist, I'm sure Barnett Newman wouldn't say he was as good as Degas. He loved Degas, actually, as I do. Once Newman came to one of the first shows I had in New York, and he said to me You know, I used to paint like this myself. And I said to him Do you mean I'm going to finish up painting blue stripes? and he laughed. He was a sweet man.

Editorial Note

Pictures by David Hockney is largely based on *David Hockney by David Hockney* which was first published in 1976. All textual matter comes from that book, which remains the standard work on the artist up to the year of its publication. Its detailed commentary on individual works still represents a unique source of information about the artist's thoughts and artistic processes. But it has always been Hockney's desire to make available an album of his most representative pictures, unencumbered by any commentary; as he stated: 'It is very good advice to believe only what an artist does, rather than what he says about his work.' This book, then, contains a representative selection of what Hockney has done up to 1979, in his painting, drawing, graphic work and, more recently, in the spectacular series, *Paper Pools*, made with coloured and pressed paper pulp.

The title for this book was suggested by Hockney himself, who has always insisted: 'I'm interested in making *pictures*.' The thematic arrangement, however, was made by me despite Hockney's slight reluctance for fear he might be thought to work in series of themes or subjects. A look at the dates of the works, however, will show that this is not the case. On the other hand, there is no doubt that he often returns to the same themes and subjects, as any artist or writer does, which not only validates a thematic arrangement but allows the viewer a fascinating glimpse of the inventive and varied ways in which the same themes are treated over time.

Grateful acknowledgment for their great help in the preparation of this book is due to: John Kasmin and Ruth Kelsey of Knoedler Kasmin Ltd, Paul Hockney and Deborah Rogers.

In the captions measurements are given first in inches then in centimetres, height before width.

Nikos Stangos

Objects and still lifes

The tea packets piled up with the cans and tubes of paint and they were lying around all the time and I just thought, in a way it's like still-life painting for me. I thought there must be other things lying around, something I could use. This is as close to pop art as I ever came. But I didn't use it because I was interested in the design of the packet. These paintings were my first attempt to put recognizable images into paintings.

Tea Painting in an Illusionistic Style, 1961.
Oil on canvas, 78 × 30 (198 × 76).

Chair and Shirt, 1972. Acrylic on canvas, 72 × 72 (183 × 183).

Suginoi Hotel, Beppu, 1971. Crayon, 14 × 17 (35·5 × 43).

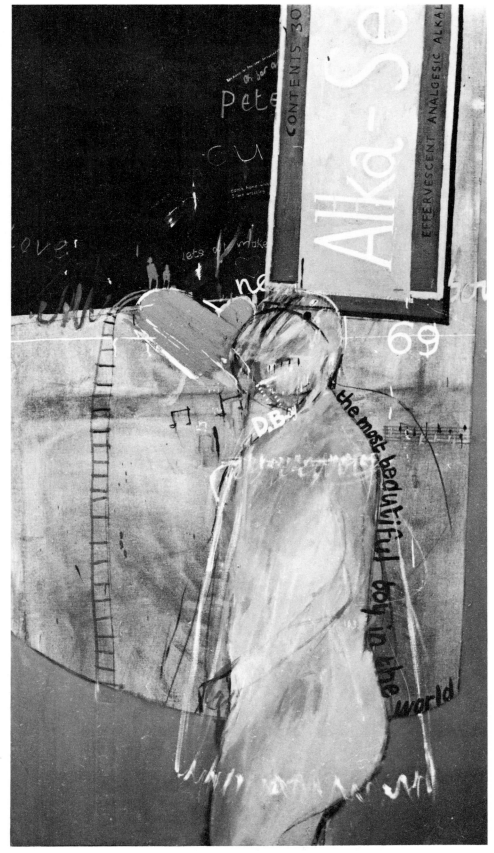

The Second Tea Painting, 1961. Oil on canvas, 61 × 36 (155 × 91).

The Most Beautiful Boy in the World, 1961. Oil on canvas, 70 × 39½ (178 × 100).

Flower, 1978. Crayon, 17 × 14 (43 × 35·5).

Still Life, Taj Hotel, 1977. Crayon, 17 × 14 (43 × 35·5).

Leeks, 1970. Crayon, 17 × 14 (43 × 35·5).

Banana, 1970. Crayon, 17 × 14 (43 × 35·5).

20

Egypt

I was interested in Egypt for several reasons, in the style, and in Egyptian painting, which in a sense is not one of the really interesting methods of painting, by any means. Egypt is fascinating, but its painting is too rigid to be really intriguing. The only thing that interested me about it was that the rules were so rigid that there's no individualism in the paintings; whoever painted them, it didn't matter; they had to obey the rules and so it all looks the same. And that interested me, the anonymous aspect of the artist, not the art. So I went to Egypt and I made a lot of drawings there. I drew everything. I went to Cairo, then Alexandria, and up to Luxor.

A Grand Procession of Dignitaries in the Semi-Egyptian Style, 1961. Oil on canvas, 84 × 144 (214 × 367).

The Second Marriage, 1963. Oil on
canvas, 77¾ × 90 (198 × 229).

The First Marriage (*A Marriage of Styles*),
1962. Oil on canvas, 77 × 60 (183 × 153).

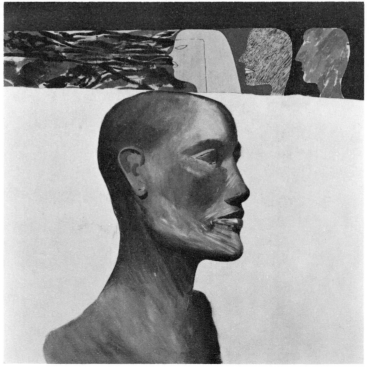

Four Heads (*Egyptian*), 1963. Oil on
canvas, 48 × 48 (122 × 122).

*Great Pyramid at Giza with Broken Head
from Thebes,* 1963. Oil on canvas, 72 × 72
(183 × 183).

The Luxor Hotel, 1978. Crayon, 14 × 17 (35·5 × 43).

The Savoy Hotel, Luxor, 1978. Crayon, 14 × 17 (35·5 × 43).

Cataract Hotel, Aswan, 1978. Crayon, 17 × 14 (43 × 35·5).

Curtains

The forms of the curtain first made me interested in it as a subject, and then it dawned on me that it could be even more interesting because it was *flat*. A curtain, after all, is exactly like a painting; you can take a painting off a stretcher, hang it up like a curtain; so a painter's curtain could be very real. All the philosophical things about flatness in a painting, if you go into it, are about reality, and if you cut out illusion then painting becomes completely 'real'. The idea of the curtains is the same thing.

Still Life with Figure and Curtain, 1963. Oil on canvas, 78 × 84 (198 × 214).

*Seated Woman Drinking Tea, Being
Served by Standing Companion,* 1963. Oil
on canvas, 78 × 84 (198 × 214).

Play within a Play, 1963. Oil on canvas and
plexiglass, 72 × 78 (183 × 198).

Closing Scene, 1963. Oil on canvas,
48 × 48 (122 × 122).

Showers

Americans take showers all the time. I knew that from experience and physique magazines. For an artist the interest of showers is obvious: the whole body is always in view and in movement, usually gracefully, as the bather is caressing his own body. There is also a three-hundred-year tradition of the bather as a subject in painting. Beverly Hills houses seemed full of showers of all shapes and sizes – with clear glass doors, with frosted glass doors, with transparent curtains, with semi-transparent curtains. They all seemed to me to have elements of luxury: pink fluffy carpets to step out on, close to the bedrooms.

Boy About to Take a Shower, 1964.
Acrylic on canvas, 36 × 36 (91 × 91).

Man Taking Shower, 1965. Acrylic on canvas, 60 × 48 (153 × 122).

Domestic Scene, Los Angeles, 1963. Oil on canvas, 60 × 60 (153 × 153).

Man Taking Shower in Beverly Hills, 1964.
Acrylic on canvas, 65½ × 65½ (167 × 167).

California

When I got to Los Angeles I didn't know a soul. People in New York said You're mad for going there if you don't know anybody and you can't drive. They said At least go to San Francisco if you want to go West. And I said No, no, it's Los Angeles I want to go to. I got into the motel, very thrilled; really, *really* thrilled, more than in New York the first time. I was so excited. I think it was partly a sexual fascination and attraction. I checked into this motel and walked on the beach and I was looking for the town; couldn't see it. And I saw some lights and I thought, that must be it. I walked two miles, and when I got there all it was was a big gas station, so brightly lit I'd thought it was the city. After I'd been there a couple of months, I went to visit some collectors. I'd never seen houses like that. And the way they liked to show them off! They would show you the pictures, the garden, the house. So then I painted a picture, *California Art Collector*. The houses I had seen all had large comfortable chairs, fluffy carpets, striped paintings and pre-Columbian or primitive sculptures and recent (1964) three-dimensional work. As the climate and the openness of houses (large glass windows, patios, etc.) reminded me of Italy, I borrowed a few notions from Fra Angelico and Piero della Francesca.

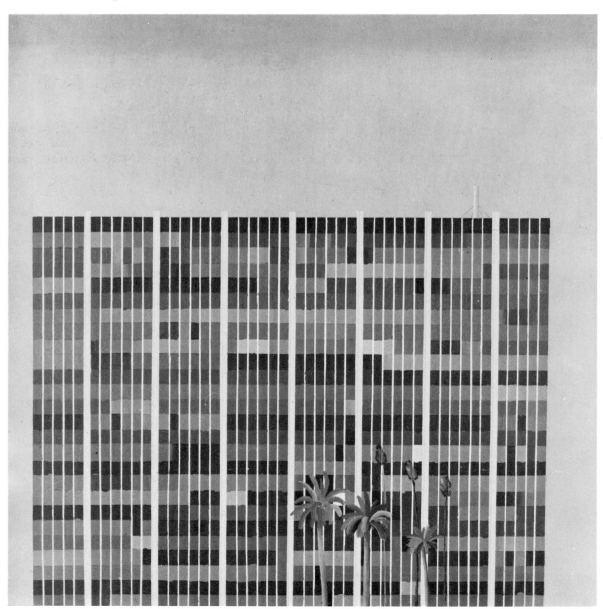

Savings and Loan Building,
1967. Acrylic on canvas,
48 × 48 (122 × 122).

Building, Pershing Square, Los Angeles,
1964. Acrylic on canvas, 58 × 58
(147 × 147).

Bank, Palm Springs, 1968. Crayon, 14 × 17
(35·5 × 43).

California Art Collector, 1964. Acrylic on
canvas, 60 × 72 (153 × 183).

Beverly Hills Housewife, 1966. Acrylic on canvas (diptych), 72 × 144 (183 × 366).

American Collectors (Fred and Marcia Weisman), 1968. Acrylic on canvas, 84 × 120 (214 × 305).

California Seascape, 1968. Acrylic on canvas, 84 × 120 (214 × 305).

A Lawn Being Sprinkled, 1967. Acrylic on canvas, 60 × 60 (153 × 153).

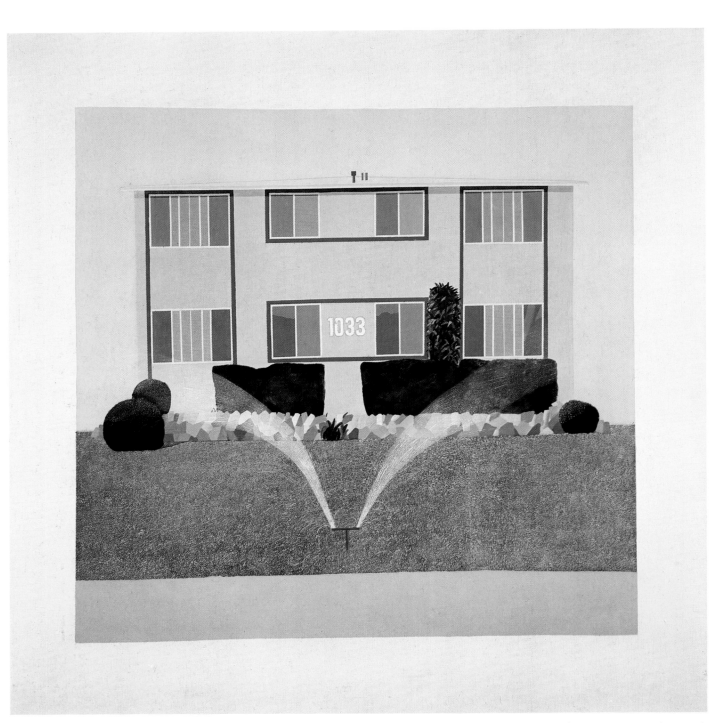

A Neat Lawn, 1967. Acrylic on canvas, 96 × 96 (244 × 244).

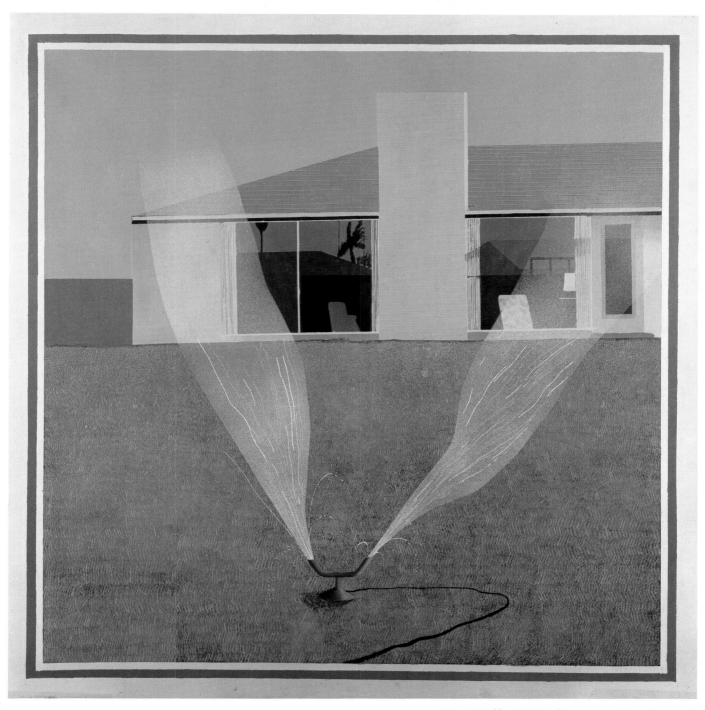

A Lawn Sprinkler, 1967. Acrylic on canvas, 48 × 48 (122 × 122).

Wilshire Boulevard, Los Angeles, 1964.
Acrylic on canvas, 36 × 24 (91 × 61).

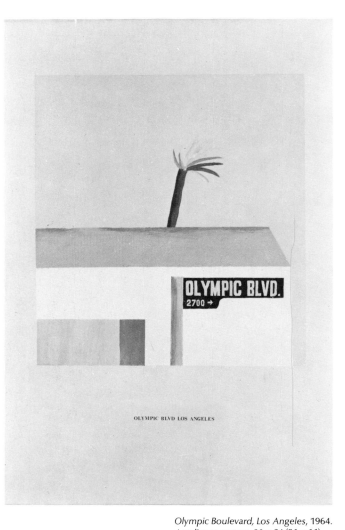

Olympic Boulevard, Los Angeles, 1964.
Acrylic on canvas, 36 × 24 (91 × 61).

Washington Boulevard, 1964. Crayon,
13½ × 10½ (34·3 × 26·7).

Los Angeles, 1967. Crayon, 14 × 17
(35·5 × 43).

House near Olympic Boulevard, 1967.
Crayon, 14½ × 16¾ (37 × 42·5).

House Behind Château Marmont, 1976.
Crayon, 14 × 17 (35·5 × 43).

De Longpre Avenue, Hollywood, 1976.
Crayon, 17 × 14 (43 × 35·5).

46

Pools and Water

The idea of painting moving water in a very slow and careful manner was (and still is) very appealing to me. In the swimming pool pictures, I had become interested in the more general problem of painting the water, finding a way to do it. It is an interesting formal problem; it is a formal problem to represent water, to describe water, because it can be anything – it can be any colour, it's movable, it has no set visual description. I just used my drawings for these paintings and my head invented. Later on, when I returned to more swimming pools – and they're painted in a different way – I took photographs of water. Water in swimming pools changes its look more than in any other form. The colour of a river is related to the sky it reflects, and the sea always seems to me to be the same colour and have the same dancing patterns. But the look of swimming-pool water is controllable – even its colour can be man-made – and its dancing rhythms reflect not only the sky but, because of its transparency, the depth of the water as well. So I had to use techniques to represent this (later I became more aware of the wetness of the surface). If the water surface is almost still and there is strong sun, then dancing lines with the colours of the spectrum appear everywhere. If the pool hasn't been used for a few minutes and there's no breeze, the look is of a single gradation of colour that follows the incline of the floor of the pool. Added to all this is the infinite variety of patterns of material that the pool can be made from.

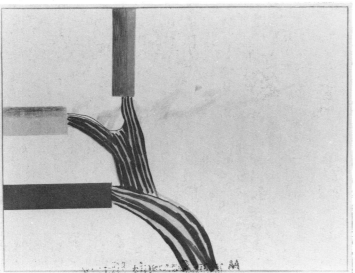

Water Entering Swimming Pool, Santa Monica, 1964. Crayon, 11 × 14 (27·5 × 35·5).

Water Pouring into Swimming Pool, Santa Monica, 1964. Lithograph on stone, in four colours, 20 × 26 (51 × 66).

Striped Water, 1965. Crayon, 13¾ × 16½ (35 × 42).

Different Kinds of Water Pouring into a Swimming Pool, Santa Monica, 1965. Acrylic on canvas, 72 × 60 (183 × 153).

The Splash, 1966. Acrylic on canvas, 72 × 72 (183 × 183).

A Bigger Splash, 1967. Acrylic on canvas, 96 × 96 (244 × 244).

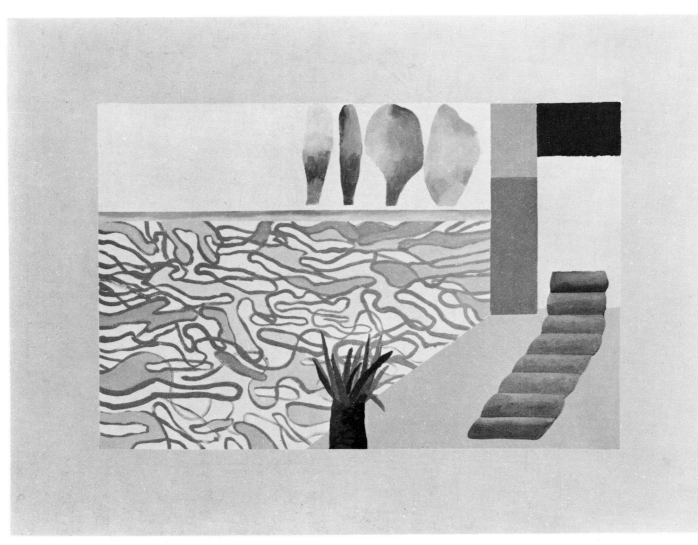

Picture of a Hollywood Swimming Pool, 1964. Acrylic on canvas, 36 × 48 (91 × 122).

Hollywood Pool and Palm Tree, 1965. Crayon, 12½ × 9¾ (32 × 25).

Swimming Pool, 1965. Pencil and crayon, 14 × 17 (35·5 × 43).

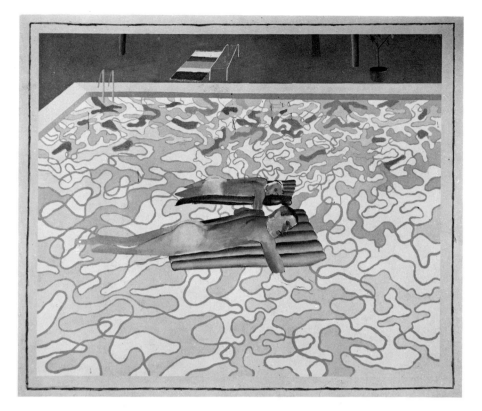

California, 1965. Acrylic on canvas,
60 × 78 (168 × 198).

Two Boys in a Pool, Hollywood, 1965.
Acrylic on canvas, 60 × 60 (153 × 153).

Peter Getting Out of Nick's Pool, 1966.
Acrylic on canvas, 84 × 84 (214 × 214).

Sunbather, 1966. Acrylic on canvas,
72 × 72 (183 × 183).

Portrait of Nick Wilder, 1966. Acrylic on canvas, 72 × 72 (183 × 183).

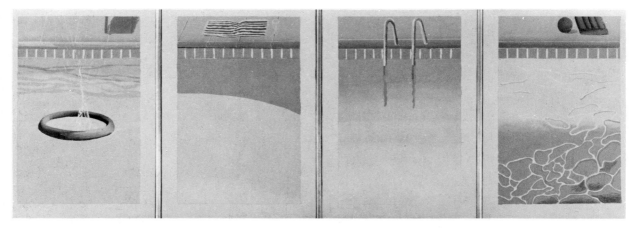

Four Different Kinds of Water, 1967.
Acrylic on canvas, 12 × 48 (31 × 122).

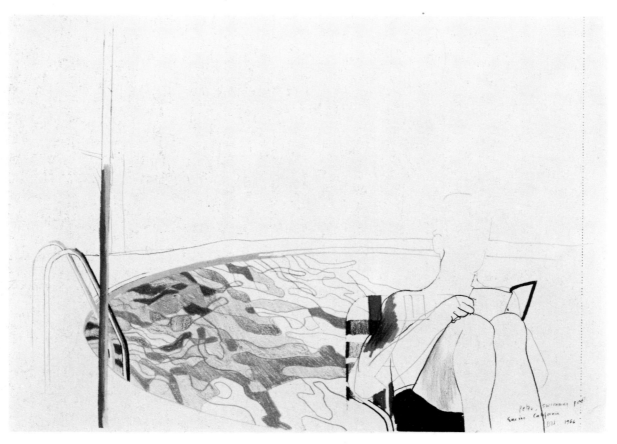

Peter, Swimming Pool, Encino, California,
1966. Crayon, 14 × 17 (35·5 × 43).

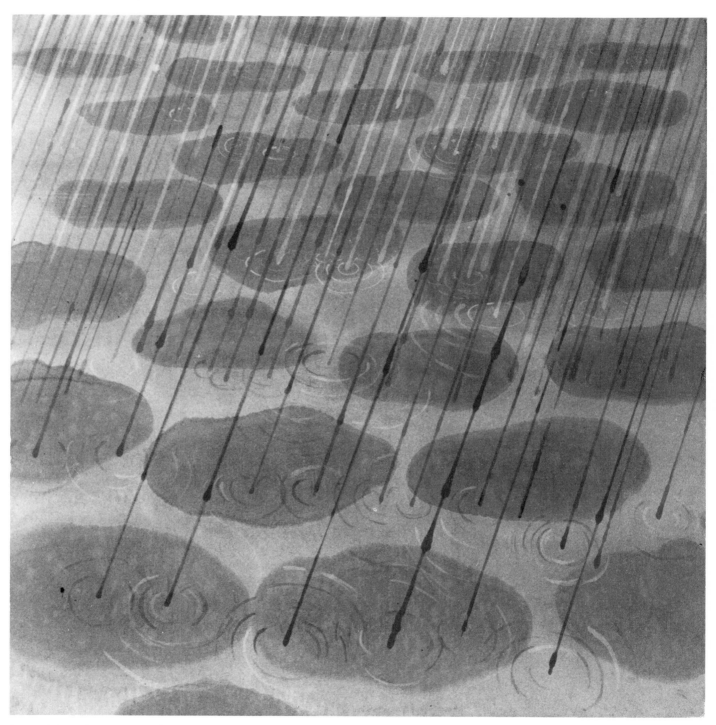

Japanese Rain on Canvas, 1972. Acrylic on canvas, 48 × 48 (122 × 122).

Pool and Steps, Le Nid du Duc, 1971.
Acrylic on canvas, 72 × 72 (183 × 183).

Portrait of an Artist (Pool with Two Figures), 1971. Acrylic on canvas, 84 × 120 (215 × 275).

Overleaf, *Pool drawing*, 1978. Ink, 14 × 17 (35·5 × 43).

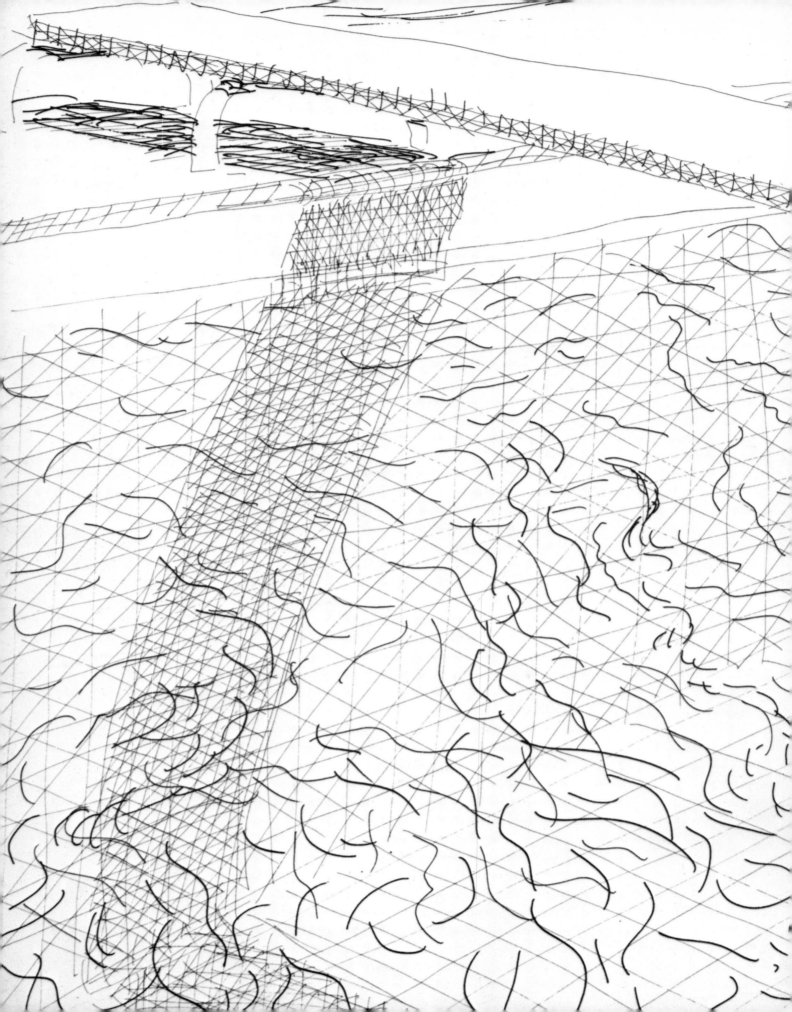

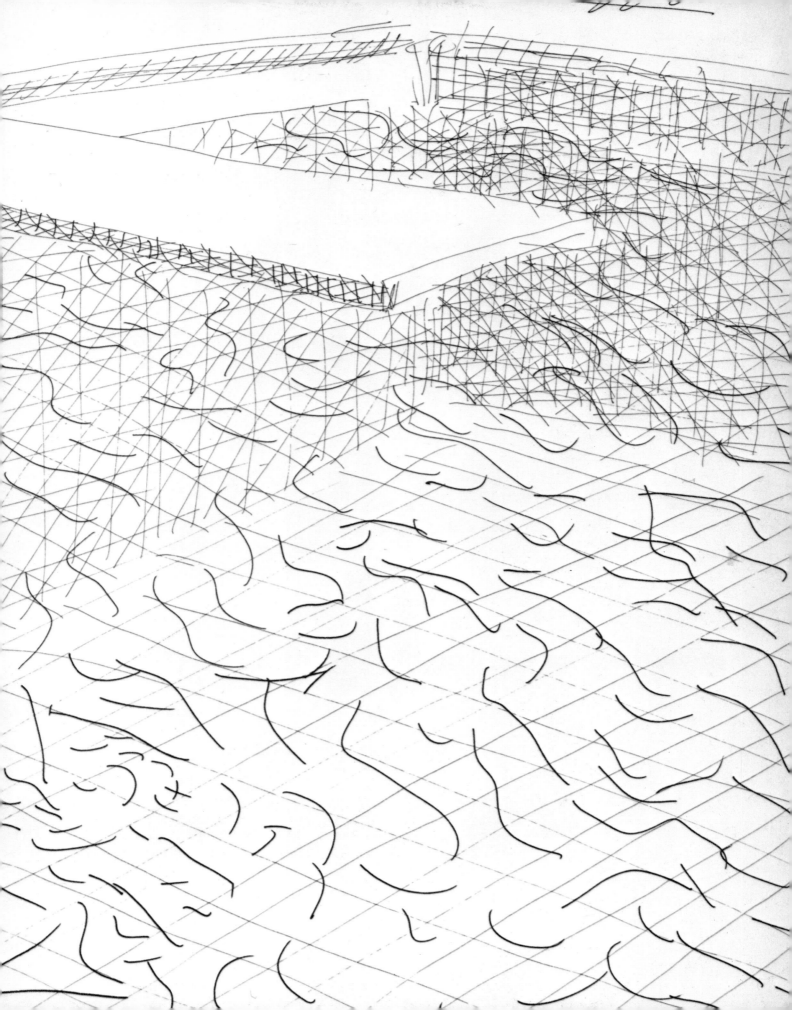

Study of Water, Phoenix, Arizona, 1976.
Crayon, 15⅞ × 19¾ (40·3 × 50).

Day Pool with Three Blues, 1978. Paper Pool 7, coloured and pressed paper pulp, 71 × 85½ (183 × 218).

Portraits

I never talk when I'm drawing a person, especially if I'm making line drawings. I prefer there to be no noise at all so I can concentrate more. You can't make a line too slowly, you have to go at a certain speed; so the concentration needed is quite strong. It's very tiring as well. If you make two or three line drawings, it's very tiring in the head, because you have to do it all at one go, something you've no need to do with pencil drawing; that doesn't have to be done in one go; you can stop, you can rub out. With line drawings, you don't want to do that. You can't rub out line, mustn't do it. It's exciting doing it, and I think it's harder than anything else; so when they succeed, they're much better drawings, often. The failure rate amongst my line drawings is still high; I'm always tearing them up and putting crosses through them, because you can't touch them up. If you draw the leg all wrong, you just have to throw it away. That's not the case with drawing on a canvas because you can alter it, move it about, draw with pencil, rub it out. And usually I'm drawing on the canvas from another drawing, so the decisions are made.

Mother (wearing black dress with white spots), 1972. Crayon, 17 × 14 (43 × 35·5).

The Artist's Father (with two watches), 1972. Ink, 17 × 14 (42 × 35·5).

64

Mother.   1972.

My Parents and Myself (unfinished state), 1975. Oil on canvas, 72 × 72 (183 × 183).

My Parents, 1977. Oil on canvas, 72 × 72 (183 × 183).

Mother, 1978. Ink, 17 × 14 (43 × 35·5).

Artist's Father, 1975. Ink, 17 × 14 (43 × 35·5).

Villa Reale, Marlia, 1973. Crayon,
14 × 17 (35·5 × 43).

Henry Geldzahler Seated, 1977.
Crayon, 14 × 17 (35·5 × 43).

Looking at Pictures on a Screen, 1977. Oil on canvas, 72 × 72 (183 × 183).

Henry, Seventh Avenue, 1972. Crayon, 17 × 14 (43 × 35·5).

Henry Sleeping, Hollywood, 1976. Crayon, 14 × 17 (35·5 × 43).

Henry Geldzahler and Christopher Scott,
1969. Acrylic on canvas, 84 × 120
(214 × 305).

Henry Asleep, 1978. Ink, 14 × 17
(35·5 × 43).

Christopher Isherwood and Don Bachardy, 1968. Acrylic on canvas, $83\frac{1}{2} \times 119\frac{1}{2}$ (212 × 304).

Le parc des sources, Vichy, 1970. Acrylic on canvas, 84 × 120 (214 × 305).

Mr and Mrs Clark and Percy, 1970–71.
Acrylic on canvas, 84 × 120 (214 × 305).

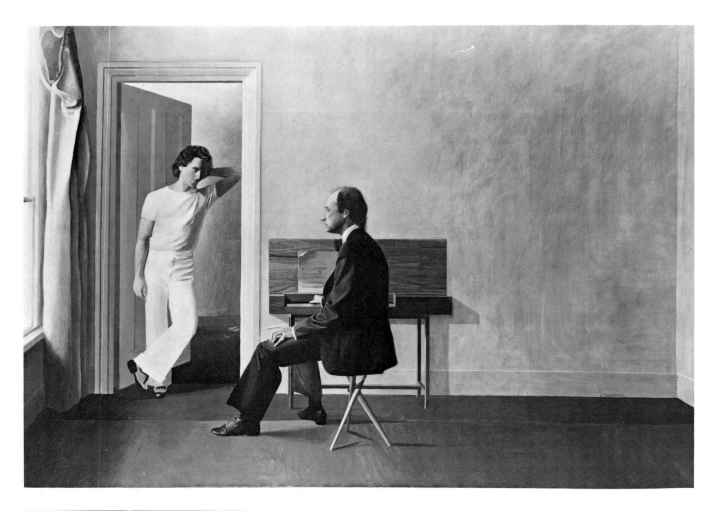

The Room, Manchester Street, 1967.
Acrylic on canvas, 96 × 96 (244 × 244).

George Lawson and Wayne Sleep
(unfinished), 1975. Acrylic on canvas,
120 × 84 (304·8 × 213·4).

Gregory Masurovsky and Shirley Goldfarb,
1974. Oil on canvas, 48 × 84 (122 × 213·4).

Celia Wearing Checked Sleeves, 1973.
Crayon, 25½ × 19¾ (65 × 50).

Celia in a Black Dress with Coloured Border, 1973. Crayon, 25½ × 19¾ (65 × 50).

Ann Upton Combing her Hair, 1979.
Acrylic on canvas, 60 × 60 (153 × 153).

Celia *(for Mo with Love)*, 1972. Crayon,
17 × 14 (43 × 35·5).

Celia (red and white dress), 1972. Crayon,
17 × 14 (43 × 35·5).

Sur la terrasse, 1971. Acrylic on canvas,
180 × 84 (457 × 214).

Peter on Balcony, 1971. Crayon, 13¾ × 10½
(35 × 27).

The Room, Tarzana, 1967. Acrylic on canvas, 96 × 96 (244 × 244).

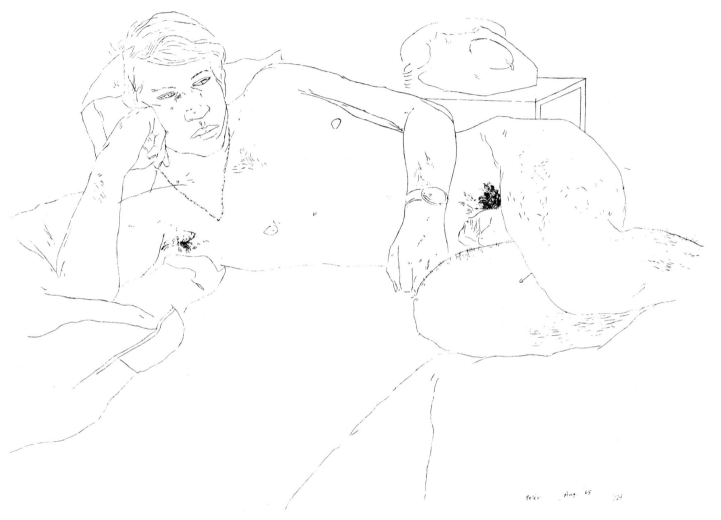

Peter, 1968. Ink, 14 × 17 (35·5 × 43).

Peter, 1972. Ink, 17 × 14 (43 × 35·5).

Peter.   Feb. 13ᵗʰ 1972

Peter, Platzel Hotel, Munich, 1972. Crayon,
17 × 14 (43 × 35·5).

Gary Farmer at Powis Terrace, 1972.
Crayon, 17 × 14 (43 × 35·5).

Nick, Grand Hotel, Calvi, 1972. Crayon,
17 × 14 (43 × 35·5).

Dr Eugen Lamb, Lucca, 1973. Crayon,
23 × 20 (60 × 51).

Henry Moore.
Cafe Royal June 23
CH.

W. H. Auden, 1968. Ink, 17 × 14 (43 × 35·5).

Henry Moore at the Café Royal, 1972. Ink, 17 × 14 (43 × 35·5).

J. B. Priestley, 1973. Ink, 17 × 14 (43 × 35·5).

Ron Kitaj outside Akademie der Künste, Vienna, 1975. Ink, 14 × 17 (35·5 × 43).

90

Ron Kitaj outside
Academie der Künste
Vienna
oct 20ᵗʰ 1975

for Ron with much love. David H

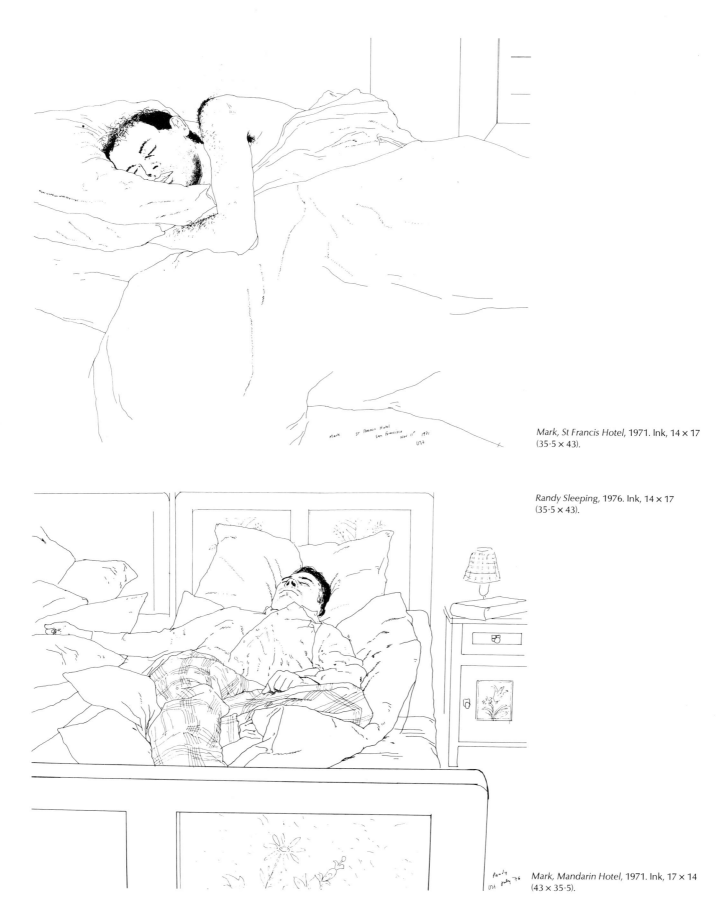

Mark, St Francis Hotel, 1971. Ink, 14 × 17
(35·5 × 43).

Randy Sleeping, 1976. Ink, 14 × 17
(35·5 × 43).

Mark, Mandarin Hotel, 1971. Ink, 17 × 14
(43 × 35·5).

Mark mandarin Hotel Hong Kong
Nov 26th 1971
DH

Nude Boy, 1978. Ink, 14 × 17 (35·5 × 43).

Kasmin Reading the Udaipur Guide, April 1977. Ink, 14 × 17 (35·5 × 43).

Maurice, 1977. Ink, 17 × 14 (43 × 35·5).

Maurice 1977

Paul, Hollywood, 1971. Ink, 17 × 14 (43 × 35·5).

Gregory Thinking in the Palatine Ruins, 1974. Ink, 25½ × 19¾ (65 × 50).

Gregory   Palatine
Roma
Dec 197

Model with Unfinished Self Portrait, 1977. Oil on canvas, 60 × 60 (152·4 × 152·4).

Detail from *Model with Unfinished Self Portrait*.

Portrait of Jean Léger, 1973. Pencil, 25½ × 19¾ (65 × 50).

Lila di Nobilis, Paris, 1973. Crayon, 25½ × 19¾ (65 × 50).

Carlos, 1975. Crayon, 25½ × 19¾ (65 × 50).

Nicky Rae, 1975. Crayon, 25½ × 19¾ (65 × 50).

Larry S., Fire Island, 1975. Ink, 14 × 17 (35·5 × 43).

Larry, Fire Island, 1975. Crayon, 14 × 17 (35·5 × 43).

Gregory, Arizona Biltmore, 1976.
Ink, 17 × 14 (43 × 35·5).

Gregory in bed, Hollywood, 1976.
Ink, 17 × 14 (43 × 33·5).

Gregory Asleep, Sunday Inn,
Houston, 1976. Ink, 14 × 17
(35·5 × 43).

Study for Louvre Window, No.2, 1974.
Crayon, 41½ × 29½ (105·4 × 74·9).

Travels

I met some English kids at a bar in Los Angeles and they said to me, Why don't you live here anymore (in 1973)? And I said, I'm living in Paris. But California is the place I always run to. Coming back to Europe you realize it's more interesting to drive around than America. America's wonderful as landscape, but every time you pull into a restaurant you know what the menu's going to be.

Two Vases in the Louvre, 1974. Oil on canvas, 72 × 60 (184 × 152·5).

Contre-jour in the French Style – Against the Day dans le style français, 1974. Oil on canvas, 72 × 72 (183 × 183).

Grand Hotel Terrace, Vittel, 1970. Crayon,
17 × 14 (43 × 35·5).

Chairs, Mamounia Hotel, Marrakesh, 1971.
Crayon, 14 × 17 (35·5 × 43).

Beach Umbrella, Calvi, 1972. Crayon, 17 × 14 (43 × 35·5).

Hotel Garden, Vichy, 1972. Acrylic on canvas, 36 × 48 (91·4 × 122).

Arlington Hotel, Hot Springs, Arkansas,
1976. Crayon, 14 × 17 (35·5 × 43).

Hotel Room, Hot Springs, Arkansas, 1976.
Crayon, 14 × 17 (35·5 × 43).

Bora Bora, 1976. Crayon, 14 × 17
(35·5 × 43).

Large Pot, Arizona Biltmore, 1976. Crayon,
14 × 17 (35·5 × 43).

111

Inventions and illustrations

I did a small strange painting, that at first people didn't understand, thought it was a bit odd. It's an invented figure, a check man, with a real still life, and the man is moving a curtain which is painted from a Fra Angelico painting, lifted straight from it. It's called *Invented Man Revealing a Still Life*. I feel that there's nothing stopping me now from painting almost anything, even just some stripes if I want; it can all fit in with a view. I've got lots of pictures I want to do, and I just want to go and invent them.

Simplified Faces (State 2), 1974. Etching, 22 × 20 (56 × 51).

(Untitled) inscribed on back *La Vie commence à quarante ans*, 1976. Acrylic on canvas, 14 × 18 (35·5 × 46·2).

Showing Maurice the Sugar Lift, 1974.
Etching, 36 × 28 (92 × 72).

Blue Guitar series: *Running Colours with Brick Mountain*, 1976. Drawing for etching in *The Man with the Blue Guitar*, coloured inks, 14 × 17 (35·5 × 43).

Invented Man Revealing Still Life, 1975. Oil on canvas, 36 × 28½ (91·4 × 72·4).

Kerby (After Hogarth) Useful Knowledge, 1975. Oil on canvas, 72 × 60 (183 × 152·4).

Catherina Dorothea Viehmann, 1969. Etching and aquatint on copper, 11 × 9 (28 × 24).

Portrait of Cavafy II, 1966. Etching and aquatint, 14 × 9 (36 × 23).

Sets

In painting I had been interested in theatrical devices, and I thought that in the theatre, the home of theatrical devices, they'd be different, they wouldn't have quite the same meaning as they do in painting, they wouldn't be contradictory – a theatrical device in the theatre is what you'd expect to find. For me, theatre design is the making of pictures on the stage.

Ubu's Banquet with Conveyor-Belt Table, 1966. Crayon, 14½ × 19½ (37 × 50).

Sketch for *The Rake's Progress*, 1975. Coloured inks and watercolour, 14 × 17 (35·5 × 43).

Drawing for the design for Roland Petit's ballet *Septentrion*, 1975. Crayon, 14 × 17 (35·5 × 43).

A set from the Glyndebourne production of *The Magic Flute*, 1978.

Acknowledgments

Numbers indicate the page on which the illustration is reproduced.
t = top   b = bottom   l = left   r = right

Ludwig Collection, Aachen 6, 106 b, 107

Harry N. Abrams Family Collection, New York 29, 35, 55, 73 t

Sir Robert Adeane, London 52 t

The Artist 64, 65, 66, 67, 68, 73 b, 76 t, 76 b, 78 t, 78 b, 79, 94 t, 106 t, 118 b, 119 b

Photo Claude Bernard 97

Bruno Bischofberger, Zurich 14

Photo Brompton 14

Photo Geoffrey Clements 33, 37 t, 38, 41, 44 tl, 54 t

Peter Coni 84

Photo A. C. Cooper 28, 29, 31, 44 tr, 48 t, 118 t

Photo Prudence Cuming Associates Ltd 6, 15 b, 16, 18, 19, 20, 21, 26 t, 26 b, 27, 36, 50, 52 br, 55, 56 b, 57, 59, 60/61, 64, 65, 66, 67, 68, 69, 70 t, 70 b, 71, 73 b, 74 b, 75, 76 t, 76 b, 81, 83, 89, 90, 91, 92 b, 93, 94 b, 95, 98, 102, 103, 104 t, 104 b, 109 b, 112 b, 114 t, 114 b, 115, 118 b, 119 t

Photo Cuming Wright-Watson 22, 35, 39 t, 39 b, 40, 43, 45 b, 48 b. 51, 54 b, 56 t, 74 t, 77, 80, 82 b, 85, 86 t, 86 b, 87 t, 87 b, 92 t, 96, 108 t, 108 b, 109 t

Dr Wilhelm Dansmann, Hamburg 44 tl

Mr and Mrs Denman, Washington, USA 38

Louisiana Museum, Denmark 58

Photo John Donat 17

The Marquess of Dufferin and Ava 21, 40, 51, 87 b

William Evans, Kansas City, USA 80, 86 t, 114 b

Mr and Mrs Fiterman 71

Fulton Art Gallery, New York 104 t

Henry Geldzahler, New York 72 t

Dr Guenther Gercken, Luetjensee, Germany 53 t

Mr and Mrs Thomas Gibson, London 87 t

Photo Guy Gravett, 119 b

Lord Hartington, London 74 b

R. B. Kitaj, London 91

Knoedler Kasmin Ltd 26 t, 26 b, 27, 52 br, 60/61, 70 b, 86 b

Jean Leger, Paris 100

Mrs M. Littman, London 82 b

British Museum, London 109 t

Mr and Mrs Ehepaar Lueg, Dortmund 36

Herbert Meyer-Ellinger, Frankfurt a.m. 42

Hans Neuendorf, Hamburg 54 b

Museum of Modern Art, New York 115

Mrs B. Organ, Wolverton 45 b

Petersburg Press 48 b

Presented by the C.A.S., London, to the National Gallery of Victoria, Melbourne 23

Private collection 32, 34, 37 t, 39, 41

Private collection, Belgium 92 b, 102

Private collection, Bradford 44 br

Private collection, Chicago 56 b, 69

Private collection, Germany 16, 17, 19, 30, 42, 53 b, 98, 105 tl, 108 t

Private collection, Hong Kong 33, 57

Private collection, Italy 37 b

Private collection, London, promised gift to National Portrait Gallery, London 74 t

Private collection, London 25, 49, 56 t, 70 t, 88, 89, 92 t, 93, 94 b, 95, 96, 103, 112 b, 118 t

Private collection, Los Angeles 22, 39 t, 47, 62

Private collection, New York City 46

Private collection, Paris 97

Private collection, Switzerland 18, 20, 31, 43, 82 t

Private collection, UK 15 t, 28, 50, 59, 77, 109 b

Private collection, USA 81, 85, 101, 105 tl, 105 tr, 105 b, 110 t, 110 b, 111 t, 111 b, 119 t

Mr and Mrs Selfe, Alabama 90

Hans Edmund Siemers, Hamburg 44 tr

Tate Gallery, London 24 t, 75

Photo Frank J. Thomas 46, 62, 72 b, 82 t, 84, 105 tl, 105 tr, 105 b, 110 t, 110 b, 111 t, 111 b

Photo R. Todd-White 32, 37 b, 45 t, 73 t, 88

Photo Kenneth Tyler 63

Albertina Museum, Vienna 114 t

Waddington Galleries, London 83

Walker Art Gallery, Liverpool 54 t

Photo John Webb 23, 24 t, 25, 30, 34, 42, 49, 52 t, 53 b

Whitworth Gallery, Manchester 108 b

Photo Rodney Wright Watson 78 t, 78 b, 101, 106 t, 106 b, 107